PILGRIMS AND PIONEERS ALWAYS

THE HISTORY OF

LEWINSVILLE PRESBYTERIAN CHURCH

1846-2013

B. Roland McElroy

Copyright 2013
Lewinsville Presbyterian Church
1724 Chain Bridge Road
McLean, Virginia 22101

1915 Photo
Lewinsville Presbyterian Church as it appeared after renovation of 1908. Note horse and buggy, hitching post, and entrance partially blocked by two trees at center.

ISBN: 978-0-9673917-8-6
Library of Congress Control Number: 2013913970

Published by
McElroy & Associates, Falls Church, Virginia 22043
Printed in the U.S.A
United Book Press, Inc.
Baltimore, Maryland

Dedication

*To the memory of all the Saints of
Lewinsville Presbyterian Church,
who have walked this path before us,
trusting only in the Word of God to guide them.*

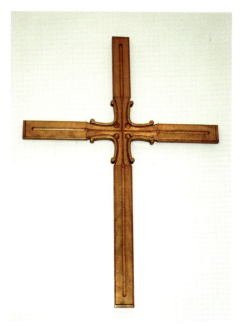

The cross in the choir loft is a gift from Dick and Jane Arnold and was dedicated when the sanctuary renovation was completed in 1991.

"Lewinsville Christians have always been pilgrims and pioneers in the faith, blazing new trails, paving the way for those who will follow."
Rev. Franklin B. Gillespie, Pastor, 1940-1948

Author's Note

The first one hundred years of Lewinsville Presbyterian Church were more about survival than anything else—surviving the Civil War, economic recessions, the Great Depression and two World Wars, to name a few. Members had little opportunity to look beyond their meager balance sheet and leaking roof until the end of World War II. When the veterans came home and started families, a population tsunami swept across the nation, and the rural community of McLean, Virginia, was not excepted.[1]

The author's sincerest hope is that the reader will discover something new, perhaps even inspirational, while exploring the extraordinary record of Lewinsville, the little white frame church that started in the wilds of Northern Virginia 167 years ago with just seventeen members.

Figure 1-Frank W. Gapp

This brief history will build upon the excellent literary work of Frank W. Gapp in 1976 and the follow up account written by Minerva Andrews and Marian O'Brien in 2000. It will explore the impact of the post-war newcomers as they moved into the neighborhoods around the church in the 1950s and exerted their influence upon the growth and development of Lewinsville's ministry in the second half of the twentieth century and the first decade of the next.

In 1948, Lewinsville member Frank Gapp began his employment with US News and World Report. "At that time, there was only one

---

[1] More than forty young men, sons of Lewinsville families, served in various branches of the Armed Forces during World War II, and all returned safely to their homes.

traffic light between our home near Tysons Corner and my office in downtown DC."[2] That one traffic light would not be lonely for long. Life was changing fast in Northern Virginia.

The little church with less than 200 members in 1948 grew to more than 1,000 members by 1975. That number tapered off and the membership was 850 to 900 for another twenty-five years. Since the turn of the last century, the number has slowly fallen and seems to have settled in the mid-600s.[3] And although smaller than it was at the height of the Baby Boom, Lewinsville remains one of the stronger churches in the National Capital Presbytery. Its present day strength is attributed to the foundation laid by thirty-seven former and current pastors, and the family of faith those pastors cultivated.

Since the 1960s, the impact of Lewinsville's congregation has been felt from the immediate neighborhood to small, isolated villages across the globe. These ministries range the full gamut of human need, especially among the elderly in the surrounding community. And it has done so in a world that is dramatically different from the one Rev. Frank Gillespie left when he departed Lewinsville in 1948.

This broad brush treatment of the Lewinsville story, undoubtedly, will omit many important details, but the author will count this brief history of Lewinsville Presbyterian Church a success if the reader comes away with a sense that God's presence is keenly felt in this place where Great Falls Street and Chain Bridge Road meet, where believers in the saving Grace of Jesus Christ have established a refuge from life's winds of adversity, a place where their faith is nurtured to maturity and generously shared with all the world.

B. Roland McElroy
October 2013

---

[2] Interview, October 1986, unused footage for film commemorating the church's 140th anniversary
[3] 660 members: Annual Report, 2012

Table of Contents

Author's Note v

Introduction xi

Chapter One: A Seed is Planted 1
    From Land Grant in 1724 to White Frame Church in 1846

Chapter Two: The Founding 7
    Physical Description of the Church in 1847
    Friendship Quilt of 1852
    Rev. Charles B. McKee (1857-1859)

Chapter Three: Civil War Struggle Splits Church 15
    Battle of Lewinsville, September 11, 1861
    Baptismal Font Missing More than a Century

Chapter Four: A Difficult Period 21
    Reparations Finally Paid
    Impact of Great Falls and Old Dominion Railroad
    Circuit Riders Keep Church Alive

Chapter Five: The Lean Years 27
    Dr. James Harvey Dunham (1923-1939)
    Rev. Franklin Brown Gillespie (1940-1948)
    A Period of Great Transition
    1952 Friendship Quilt

Chapter Six: End of an Era, Beginning of Another 35
    Rev. James Lundquist (1948-1953)
    Dr. Howard Newman (1954-1957)
    Rev. John Graham (1957-1969)

Chapter Seven: Beyond These Walls 47
    Rev. Gary George Pinder (1968-2005)
    Rev. William J. Tatum (1971-1977)
    Lewinsville Retirement Residence is Born
    A Co-Pastorate Created
    Rev. John Preston Smith (1979-1985)
    Marie T. Lewis
    Music at Lewinsville
    J. Franklin Clark
    Expansion and Renovation Begun in 1989
    Financial Crisis Averted
    Lewinsville East
    Roots of Lewinsville's Annual Summer Mission Project
    One Hundred Mission Programs

Chapter Eight: Christian Formation 67
    Constantly Evolving
    Education Redefined
    Reformed Institute of Metropolitan Washington Established in 2003

Chapter Nine: Carry One Another's Burdens 73
    Presbyterian Women
    Deacons Reconstituted
    ChristCare Groups Established
    Social Group Connectivity
    Second Saturday Set

Chapter Ten: Decently and In Order 79
First Up, Then Down
Session of Twenty-Eight Elders
Foundation Established in 1985
1846 Covenant Society Created in 2009

Chapter Eleven: That Vision Thing 83
Journey for Discernment Adopted in 2005
Mission/Vision Statements Adopted in 2013

Chapter Twelve: A New Millennium Begins 89
Digital Age Arrives
Major Personnel Changes
Chesterbrook Residences Opened

Chapter Thirteen: Making New Disciples 103

Chapter Fourteen: Saints and Sinners 107

Afterword – Serving Christ in a Nanotube World 111

Acknowledgements 115

Appendix I 117
First Trustee: Commodore Thomas ap Catesby Jones

Appendix II 121
History of Lewinsville Organs; History of Lewinsville Bells

Appendix III 127
"Concerning Our Church," November 18, 1956

Appendix IV 131
Lewinsville Tapestry

Appendix V 135
  Musical Productions and Cantatas

Appendix VI 139
  Return of Baptismal Font; Return of Pulpit Lamp

Appendix VII 145
  Summer Mission Project – Trip History (1990-2013)

Appendix VIII 151
  Pastors, Associate Pastors, Assistant Pastors, Co-Pastors, Stated Supplies

Appendix IX 153
  Milestone Celebrations

Appendix X 155
  Clerks of Session

Appendix XI 157
  1852 Friendship Quilt

Memorials 160

Introduction

Lewinsville was not the first Presbyterian Church to be established in or near the Nation's Capital, but it was a singularly determined rock of Reformed Tradition that struggled and scratched its way into a permanent faith presence at Barrett's Crossroads.[4] That fact will become imminently clear by the time a stopping point is reached in this account of Lewinsville's history.

---

[4] Old Presbyterian Meeting House in Alexandria (often referred to as George Washington's Church) was founded in 1772, and First Presbyterian of Capitol Hill in Washington, DC, was founded in 1795. Its name was later changed when it became National Presbyterian Church.

Lewinsville Church has suffered many kicks to the shin over the decades but always recovered to continue its Christian ministry. It overcame dissension and division created by the Civil War. It escaped abandonment when the trolley chose a path through McLean, bypassing Lewinsville. Even the Great Depression and two world wars could not discourage the faithful of Lewinsville who, no doubt, kept repeating, "Where two or three are gathered together…"

**

Chapter One
A Seed is Planted

The history of the little frame church at Barrett's Crossroads began with a simple bequest from the will of Elizabeth Jones in 1822. Elizabeth was the sister of Commodore Thomas ap Catesby Jones, who is generally credited with founding the church. Indeed, he did see to the physical construction of the church in 1846, but it was his sister, Elizabeth, who took the initial step toward its founding by stipulating in her will that four acres of her land holdings be set aside for

the establishment of a church and church yard in the settlement of Lewinsville.

"...the time has passed for us to have our own house of worship at Lewinsville."

"The nearest Presbyterian Church is in Alexandria," Elizabeth wrote in her diary, a clear reference to the Old Presbyterian Meeting House, erected in 1772. "The time has passed for us to have our own house of worship at Lewinsville." Elizabeth knew exactly how long it took her family to make the trip to Alexandria, and she wanted no part of the rough ride to Alexandria. She certainly had no desire to venture into the District of Columbia to find a church.

She was not the first to make note of the absence of Presbyterian churches in Northern Virginia. In 1812, when Elizabeth was twenty-six years of age, a committee of citizens reported to the Presbytery of

Baltimore that the area "southwest of the Potomac invited attention."[5] The Presbytery asked the Reverend William Maffitt, who was teaching at a school in nearby Langley, to explore the potential for a church in Northern Virginia.[6] He was well known to the Presbytery through his service as Stated Supply to several churches within its jurisdiction, including the church at Bladensburg, Maryland, where he was ordained.

The first meetings to discuss forming a church were held in Rev. Maffitt's McLean home, *Salona*.[7] Elizabeth Lee Jones often attended those meetings with her parents, Major Catesby Jones and her mother, Lettice. Her brother, Thomas ap Catesby Jones, was off serving his country as a lieutenant in the US Navy when the first meetings were held. At *Salona*, "Miss Betty," as she was affectionately known, heard

---

[5] Franklin Brown Gillespie, *A Brief History of Lewinsville Presbyterian Church*, p. 4, Prepared for the 100th anniversary of the church in 1946. Early Session minutes for the period preceding 1922 have been lost. Gillespie's research led him to minutes of Presbytery, historical records of the General Assembly, Library of Congress, Fairfax County Courthouse, and US Archives. At the Library of Congress, he reviewed twenty volumes, 200 pages each, of Presbytery notes and minutes, all handwritten. In a few instances the memories of the elderly in the 1946 congregation were tapped by Rev. Gillespie to fill in a few gaps.

[6] Rev. Maffitt was highly regarded by the several congregations he served as Stated Supply before moving to the Langley/McLean area. His education was the result of studying with Presbyterian clergy who lived near his home in Cecil County, Maryland. Such an education was not uncommon at the time.

[7] The original house is preserved at 1214 Buchanan Street, McLean, Virginia, and is listed on the National Register of Historic Places. Built in 1812, *Salona* was, for many years, the home of Revolutionary War hero, Henry "Light Horse Harry" Lee.

sermons from Rev. Maffitt, and on occasion, two other ministers named Tustin and Harrison from Alexandria.[8]

"Miss Betty" noted in correspondence with friends that while there was plenty of enthusiasm for a church, a consensus could not be reached on a site or a funding source. Informal meetings continued at *Salona* and Elizabeth continued her participation. But, at every opportunity, she let it be known that she was disappointed in the lack of progress toward the establishment of a church in the Lewinsville community.

Elizabeth Jones died in 1822, at the age of thirty-five, and according to one source, "she died at the seat of her brother, Captain Thomas ap Catesby Jones."[9] No cause of death has been found. Her will made it abundantly clear that she wished to have a church built on a portion of the land she had inherited from her Turberville roots.

> *"…dedicated to the uses and purposes of divine worship in such manner and subject to such rules as shall…be from time to time prescribed by the Rev. William Maffitt…"*[10]

Regrettably, Elizabeth's wishes remained in limbo while the courts sought to untangle debts associated with the estate of her deceased uncle, Troilus Lewin Turberville. Troilus was the first of three heirs to die. He died an alcoholic in 1803. The other children named as heirs in the John Turberville will were: Laetitia ("Lettice") Corbin Jones, née, Turberville and Martha Corbin Ball, née, Turberville. When "Lettice" died in 1812, a portion of the Turberville estate fell to her daughter, Elizabeth Lee Jones. When Elizabeth died in 1822, her land reverted to the estate of her mother, Lettice, and it was immediately embroiled in a

---

[8] Ibid., *A Brief History*, p. 4
[9] Extract from the reading of Last Will and Testament (dated 16th of April, 1822), of Miss Elizabeth Lee Jones, formerly of Northumberland, afterwards of Fairfax, in Virginia.
[10] Fairfax County, Virginia, Will Book N-1, p. 49; Fairfax County, Virginia, Deed Book V-2, p. 85. Elizabeth's will lists the names of eight other Presbyterian ministers with the freedom to "prescribe" worship on her land.

legal fight over the debts of Troilus. (See chart on next page for clarification of the lineage.)

The remaining original heir to the John Turberville estate, Martha Corbin Ball, picked up the challenge to defend the estate from creditors. She did so with the able assistance of her husband, Dr. Mottrom Ball and her nephew, Thomas ap Catesby Jones, who had returned from the War of 1812 with the rank of Commodore.[11] The legal proceedings concluded in 1830 when Commodore Jones, Martha and her husband, Dr. Ball, agreed to pay the remaining indebtedness of Troilus. The path to building a church on Elizabeth's land was finally cleared of all obstacles.

In the 1830 court decree, Dr. Ball, his wife Martha, and Commodore Jones became owners of Elizabeth's land, but, for some inexplicable reason, there was no movement toward construction of a church until after Dr. Ball's death in 1842. Commodore Jones and Martha Ball donated the necessary acreage to fulfill Elizabeth's wishes in 1846, twenty-four years *after* the first reading of her will.

---

[11] See **Appendix I** for account of Jones' involvement in the War of 1812.

From Land Grant in 1724 to White Frame Church in 1846

Thomas Fairfax, 6th Lord Fairfax of Cameron (1693-1781). In 1724, Lord Fairfax granted 3,402 acres to Virginia's George Lee Turberville of Westmoreland, Virginia.

George Lee Turberville (1694-1742), left the land to his only son, John Turberville.

John Turberville (1737-1799), bequeathed the future church acreage to three heirs:

1. Laetitia ("Lettice") Corbin Turberville (1763-1812). She married, at age fifteen, Major Catesby Jones. Of their several children, two helped established Lewinsville Presbyterian Church:
    a. Elizabeth Lee Jones (1786-1822). Her 1822 will set aside four acres for a church.
    b. Thomas ap Catesby Jones (1790-1858). He later joined the US Navy and achieved the rank of Commodore before retiring to Virginia.
2. Martha Corbin Turberville (1778-1865). She married Dr. Mottrom Ball in 1800.
3. Troilus Lewin Turberville (1780-1803). He died an alcoholic, at the youthful age of twenty-three, leaving many unpaid debts.

**

Chapter Two
The Founding

The countryside surrounding Washington, DC in 1846 was decidedly rural and sparsely populated. Small dairy farms, often separated by miles and miles of dense woods, dotted the landscape. Little more than wagon trails marked the principal travel routes in the area. Names like Chain Bridge Road, Courthouse Road, Gallows Road and Great Falls Street left little doubt about their purpose or destination. Such was the physical environment in which Lewinsville Church was born.

On October 17, 1846, Lewinsville Presbyterian Church was officially established by the Presbytery of Winchester. In the middle of winter, January 3, 1847, with seventeen members attending, the official dedication took place.[12]

Figure 2-Winter, 1941

---

[12] Among the seventeen in attendance were: Commodore and Mrs. Thomas Jones, Martha Corbin Turberville Ball, Miss Lucy Ball, Mr. Amzi Coe, Mr. Archibald Sherwood, Mr. and Mrs. Gilbert, Mr. and Mrs. Osbourn, Mr. and Mrs. Ives, and Mr. Beard. The names were recalled by Commodore Jones' granddaughter, Miss Martha C. Jones, many years after the dedication.

The white frame building, erected at a cost of $650, adjoined a cemetery, previously established on the Ball family property.[13] A manse, stable and schoolhouse soon followed. Rev. Levi H. Christian was called in 1846 to be the first pastor and agreed to preach for $200 a year.

Physical Description of the Church in 1847

The rectangular church, a white-frame colonial building, was approximately fifty by thirty-five feet, a scale typical of the plain meeting house style utilized by many reformed protestant churches at the time, especially in rural areas.

There was a small vestibule at the entrance with a balcony above it. The one room was supported by a substantial foundation of native stone. The structure itself was of virgin timber harvested from the surrounding forest. Inside, two potbelly stoves sat in opposite corners at the rear of the building. The congregation sat on straight back wooden pews. From the entrance, one could see a platform at the far end, which raised the pulpit and pulpit furniture about a foot, enough to grant everyone an unobstructed view of the preacher and a small choir.

"…it was severely plain."

Interior walls consisted of plaster on a simple lathe. The windows were approximately nine feet in height, and consisted of three sections of hand blown glass. A glance around the room would reveal no fancy ornamentation of any kind. "It was severely plain," as one local described it. Outside, on each side of the entrance, a couple of crude hitching posts were installed.

As with many churches in the South before the Civil War, Lewinsville Church had a balcony over the vestibule set aside for "servants" (euphemism for slaves). Some churches provided an outside entrance to the balcony via a ladder. At Lewinsville, a narrow stairway

---

[13] The first known burial occurred in 1846 when a young minister, Rev. Samuel S. Hawley, 31, was buried there. Seven more burials occurred in 1846.

inside facilitated slave access to the balcony.[14] Griffin Dobson, slave of Commodore Jones, was one of those who regularly accompanied his master to church. Another slave, Belinda Brown, who worked for the Ball and Judkins families, is buried in the Ball family plot at Lewinsville.[15]

Rev. Levi H. Christian, the first called pastor served two years. He was replaced by Rev. F.N. Whaley, a licentiate under the care of the Winchester Presbytery. Rev. Whaley was given the daunting task of serving Lewinsville while reserving half of his time for church development in the rest of Fairfax County.

> **Commodore Jones died in 1858, at age sixty-eight. His aunt, Martha Ball, died in 1865, at age eighty-seven. Martha's only daughter, Lucy Waring Ball, was active in the church until her death in 1862. Organizing pastor, Rev. William Maffitt died in 1828. He and Commodore Jones are buried in the Lewinsville cemetery, as are several descendants of Dr. Mottrom Ball and his wife, Martha.**

Rev. B.F. Bittinger followed Whaley in 1852. He also attempted to establish new churches in the city of Fairfax and Falls Church. By 1856, Lewinsville had grown to sixty-nine congregants.[16] The small church Rev. Bittinger was able to establish at Fairfax withered away and was soon dissolved by Presbytery. Its few remaining members were turned over to Lewinsville.

Friendship Quilt of 1852

During the pastorate of Rev. Bittinger, an "attractive and comfortable manse was erected on the Church property."[17] A Friendship

---

[14] Slave balcony was removed in the renovation of 1908.
[15] Ibid., *A Brief History*, p. 28, Marker: "In loving memory of Belinda Brown, colored, the faithful friend and nurse in the Ball and Judkins families prior to and during the Civil War and the dark days of Reconstruction. Faithful unto death."
[16] Ibid., p. 5
[17] Ibid.

Quilt was presented to Rev. Bittinger when he arrived in 1852, containing 108 names, carefully recorded for posterity in indelible ink. Undoubtedly, the 108 names included participating youth from the Sunday School as well as registered members of the church. Regrettably, the quilt was lost for many years. By chance, a member of the Lewinsville congregation spied it in a missionary barrel, about to be shipped overseas by one of the Washington area churches. She recognized the quilt immediately and promptly returned it to Lewinsville.[18] Unfortunately, due to its fragile condition, the Bittinger quilt is no longer displayed. [19]

Figure 3-1852 Friendship Quilt: 8'9" x 7'7"

Figure 4-"Thomas ap Catesby Jones, USN, Sharon"

---

[18] Slide presentation by Frank Gapp, delivered October 1986 as part of the 140th anniversary celebration.
[19] See **Appendix XI** for additional photos of 1852 Quilt

Rev. Charles B. McKee (1857-1859)

For many years, it was thought that a written record of the early church was lost, or perhaps never existed. Imagine the surprise of Rev. John Graham when, in the mid-1960s, he opened his mail to find an envelope addressed to "The First Presbyterian Church, Lewinsville, Va." Inside was the personal diary of Rev. C.B. McKee, Pastor of Lewinsville from 1857 to 1859. The diary was discovered in a trash heap near Newark, New Jersey, and forwarded by an unknown person, possibly a descendant of McKee. The McKee diary revealed much about the challenges facing a rural pastor in the mid-nineteenth century—from the minutiae of daily life to bitter debates about church doctrine.

From the start, McKee worried about everything. He was a poor man who did not own a horse so he walked everywhere. He seemed obsessed with his personal compensation and referred to it frequently in his diary, always making careful note of agreements reached with the elders regarding his compensation.

"…Today my labors & salary commence…$500 a year = $125 per quarter/$41.66 2/3 per month/$9.61 per week/$1.37 per day."[20]

There is evidence that he supplemented his income by teaching children of his neighborhood whose parents could afford his fee ($10 per child, per quarter). His diary also contained his personally concocted home remedies. One formula showed how to use gum arabic[21] to make a

---

[20] Diary of the Rev. C.B. McKee, June 28, 1857. All diary entries are for 1857.
[21] Sometimes called acacia gum; an extract from the bark of an acacia tree

cough medicine which he labeled, Brown Mixture. Apparently, he had occasion to use it often because he kept that formula at the front of his diary.

McKee's pastorate was marked by heated differences of opinion on the notion that women should be given a stronger role in church leadership. Consider the secular environment: Susan B. Anthony and Elizabeth Cady Stanton were lecturing far and wide on women's rights. In New York, Amelia Bloomer was urging women to wear an article of clothing she designed and named, "bloomers." Her advertisements described them as "more practical – and healthier, too."[22]

> ***"…fine for women to pray but they should not attempt to lead prayer in public meetings…"***

And at Lewinsville, someone had the temerity to introduce a woman to lead prayer. It was all too much for one elder, Amzi Coe of Falls Church, who immediately offered to resign his eldership. Coe was an influential member of the church, especially since his membership dated back to its founding. Rev. McKee counseled Coe not to act in haste, and expressed the view that surely the idea "would soon die out."[23] In his diary, he wrote that it was "fine for women to pray but they should not attempt to *lead* prayer in public meetings" as that would be a violation of the Apostle Paul's list of prohibitions. McKee made no further mention of the issue in his diary, and thus it is not clear how the matter was resolved.

Perhaps McKee's most significant contribution to the community came in the form of his aggressive lobbying for a post office to be established at Lewinsville. His many months of persistent petitioning finally bore fruit. He received word on October 3, 1857, that a post office would be opened within the week. The little post office also housed a general store. It was located directly across Great Falls Street

---

[22] Advertisement in "The Lily," 1851 advocacy publication, owned by Amelia Bloomer
[23] Ibid., Diary of Rev. C. B. McKee

from the church, and served the community until 1911 when both Langley and Lewinsville lost their post offices to a burgeoning population in McLean.[24]

Rev. McKee resigned his pastorate in 1859 and moved to Georgetown. When the Civil War broke out, Union troops occupied the church, and the church had no pastor for about four years. An occasional visiting pastor filled the pulpit, and even McKee came out from Georgetown several times. McKee makes little reference in his diary to membership during his tenure, but it is important to note that membership grew to eighty-three in 1858, *the highest recorded number of congregants until 1939.*[25]

**

---

[24] Growth in McLean was a direct result of the trolley line that ran through the heart of McLean, connecting Rosslyn and Great Falls. Today's Old Dominion Drive marks the path of the trolley line through McLean.
[25] Ibid., *A Brief History*, p. 6

Chapter Three
Civil War Struggle Splits Church

Lewinsville Church grew steadily through the 1850s, but its history, like the history of almost every rural church below the Mason-Dixon Line was changed forever when the Civil War erupted in 1861. Lewinsville members reluctantly accepted a state of war as a way of life, and all religious activity in the community ceased for the duration. Passions within the church ran high on both sides of the secession question.

Just a month after the secession initiative was adopted by the Virginia legislature, Lewinsville residents were presented with the ballot question and given the opportunity to decide whether to repeal or ratify the secession proposal. On Thursday, May 23, 1861, the Lewinsville precinct voted 86 to 37 in favor of remaining in the Union.[26] Voting to reject the bill of secession were Jonathan Magarity, James Frizzell, Mason Shipman, James and Jackson Magarity—all men of considerable influence in the community and members of Lewinsville Church.[27]

Battle of Lewinsville, September 11, 1861

The little community of Lewinsville was unable to escape the conflict because its location offered a strategic point for the defense of the Capital against military units of the Confederacy. This became

---

[26] Gapp, Frank W., *A Concise History*, p. 13
[27] Language of the Bill: "An Ordinance to repeal the ratification of the Constitution of the United States of America, by the State of Virginia, and to resume all the rights and powers granted under said Constitution."

evident in 1861 when Union forces conducted a reconnaissance mission to Lewinsville.

> "...Colonel Isaac Stevens, 79th New York Infantry, left Camp Advance near Fort Marcy, taking First Lieutenant Orlando Poe of the Topographical Engineers and an aggregate force of 1,800, to examine the vicinity around Lewinsville as a possible site for permanent occupation. They were there for several hours while Rebels observed at a distance. When the survey was finished a bugle sounded recall. As the Union forces lined up in columns to form a return to camp, Confederate forces, led by Colonel J.E.B. Stuart, Commanding Officer, First Virginia Cavalry, opened a destructive fire with guns and cannons. Although they experienced heavy shelling, the Union soldiers were able to silence the enemy guns, but not before lives were lost on both sides, mainly the Union. Even though there were further skirmishes in and about Lewinsville, this was the main event and became known as the Battle of Lewinsville."[28]

Figure 5 on the next page is a copy of an engraved image from the *Illustrated London News* depicting officers saluting the wounded men after the battle of Lewinsville in Virginia, September 11, 1861. (Published in the *Illustrated London News (ILN)*, October 12, 1861.)[29]

---

[28] Carole L. Herrick, *Images of America, McLean, Virginia*, 2011, p. 37
[29] Displayed in St. Andrews Hall, Lewinsville Church, actual "tear sheet" from newspaper, other news stories are printed on back of illustration

Civil War Struggle Splits Church || 17

Figure 5-The Battle of Lewinsville

Most interesting was the perspective of the incident from the view of both Confederate and Union troops.

A Confederate perspective:
Col. J.E.B. Stuart, commanding the 13th Virginia Volunteers, wrote in his official account, "I intended to surprise them Yankees and I succeeded entirely."

Later, Colonel Stuart wrote to General Longstreet:
"...a few shots from Rosser's section at a cluster of the enemy a quarter of a mile off put the entire force of the enemy into full retreat, exposing their entire column to flank fire from our piece."

A brief Union account from records of the 3rd Regiment, Vermont Volunteers:
"On September 11, the regiment participated in a reconnaissance to and beyond Lewinsville, Virginia, where it engaged Confederate skirmishers. Returning to the camp, the

regiment came under fire from Rosser's battery. A shell fell within the ranks of Company C, killing Private Amos Meserve, mortally wounding William H. Colburn, and injuring five others."

Personal observation of Colonel Isaac Stevens:
"(Lewinsville) has great natural advantages, is easily defensible, will require but a small amount of ordnance, and should be permanently occupied without delay."

Both sides fought bravely and both sides claimed victory at the Battle of Lewinsville. The only thing certain is that the little church at Lewinsville lost that day. For two years, it was occupied by Union forces and became part of the Union defense that encircled the capital.

Baptismal Font Missing for More than a Century

After the war, members gave little thought to finding any of the furnishings taken from the church. They assumed all were stolen or destroyed during the military occupation. One item survived, however, a porcelain baptismal font. The font was rescued by Wisconsin nurse, Eliza T. Wilson, who accompanied the Fifth Wisconsin regiment when they occupied the grounds. When she saw the church filled with straw and learned that federal troops had instructions to burn the church should it be overrun by Confederate troops, she hid the font among her belongings and ultimately took it back to Wisconsin. After the war, the font was displayed in the Downsville Lumber Museum where Lewinsville member, Barbara Kriss, discovered it 133 years later. In perfect

Figure 6-Original Baptismal Font on display today

condition, it was generously returned to Lewinsville, May 12, 1996, just in time for Lewinsville's 150th anniversary.[30]

There is no record of what was used as a baptismal font following the loss of the original porcelain font. The first mention of a new baptismal bowl was in 1891 when Mrs. Henry Pierce Viles, a Washington artist and friend of the Lewinsville pastor, gave the church an engraved silver baptismal font. The silver bowl was used until the mid to late 1970s when another memorial gift made possible a stand-alone baptismal font designed to complement the rest of the chancel furniture.

Figure 7-The Steel Family, 2011

Figure 8-New baptismal font, dedicated April 2013

In 2013, a newly designed font was approved by Session and dedicated April 14. Nancy Donnelly of the Washington Glass Studio was commissioned to create the fused glass bowl, the central feature of the font. "Lewinsville leadership wanted to see the water in action," Ms. Donnelly wrote in her blog. "(Lewinsville) wanted a big bowl, nice shallow curve so the water would be 'scoopable,' clear glass with a wavelet pattern in blues, darker in the center and fading toward the rim."[31]

**

---

[30] See **Appendix VI** for full story of the missing font
[31] Blog, Washington Glass School, posting of April 11, 2013

Chapter Four
A Difficult Period

In the half century following the Civil War, the church struggled mightily to sustain its membership. Indeed, many churches in the South experienced similar difficulties, the result of split allegiances during the War and attrition caused by casualties of war. Nevertheless, members petitioned Presbytery of the Potomac less than six months following the war for support. By the end of 1866, members had repaired most of the physical damage to the church, but the membership was about half its pre-war numbers. Presbytery declared Lewinsville a missionary church, and home-mission funds were designated to pay half of the pastor's stipend each year.

No less than thirteen pastors served Lewinsville during the years leading up to 1900, six of them as Stated Supplies and two as visiting preachers. Attendance was so poor, Rev. Harrison Clarke felt it necessary to ask Presbytery to dissolve his pastoral relationship. Conditions were such that, in 1870, one pastor appearing before Presbytery, urged those gathered to adopt a motion to permit the occupancy of the church by the Methodists. Action was deferred until the next meeting, at which the Presbytery firmly denied the motion and resolved to "supply the pulpit at Lewinsville with the Stated means of Grace as far as possible."[32] Lewinsville was not completely able to sustain itself financially until 1908.

In the middle of many challenges to its survival, the faithful at Lewinsville "seeded" two additional churches from their membership

---

[32] Ibid., *A Brief History*, p. 10

base. The result was the establishment of Falls Church Presbyterian in 1873 and Vienna Presbyterian in 1871.[33] These were the "lean years," according to Rev. John Brown who served Lewinsville as Pastor for two of those leans years, 1873 to 1875. When Vienna was "seeded," Lewinsville's membership dropped to just ten.[34]

> *"...at present the spiritual state of the congregation is one of much progress..."*

Through the latter half of the nineteenth century, the small congregation worked hard to rebuild every facet of the ministry they started. *A History of the Churches of Washington City Presbytery*, written in 1888, made note of Lewinsville's progress: "At present the spiritual state of the congregation is one of much promise, the membership having recently more than doubled." But records show church membership was only thirty-six in 1888 and Sunday School membership only forty.

Reparations Finally Paid

Thirty-six years after surrender documents were signed at Appomattox Courthouse, a "Bill for the Relief of Lewinsville Presbyterian Church" was introduced in the Congress (December 10, 1901). A claim for reparations had been made by the church immediately after the Civil War, but payment was delayed.

Some speculated that the delay was due to an investigation to determine if the church had demonstrated enough loyalty to the Union during the war. After all, The Tucker Act of 1887 stipulated that no reparations would be made to churches that sided with the Confederacy.

---

[33] Ibid., p. 11. Lewinsville also "seeded" Immanuel and Chesterbrook of McLean, and First Presbyterian of Arlington. First Presbyterian of Arlington was, for a long time, known as Ballston Presbyterian. A Lewinsville elder, Miles C. Munson, helped organize the Ballston church. He is the only elder with the distinction of serving as elder at Lewinsville, Falls Church, Ballston, and Arlington Presbyterian Churches.

[34] Ibid., *A Brief History*, p. 11, and *The Church at Lewinsville*, p. 21

A Difficult Period | 23

It was well known that many Lewinsville members had joined the rebellion. There is also evidence that while "most ministers were faithful,"[35] some were found to have cooperated with the South. One of them, "Rev. Pugh (of the Potomac Presbytery) had been arrested as a Rebel lieutenant of Artillery and was considered a dangerous man to the United States Government."[36]

When the US Court of Claims finally convened on the matter in 1903, Miss Martha C. Jones, daughter of Commodore Jones, then in her sixties, testified to the physical damage suffered by the church:

> *"...the parsonage barn was totally destroyed, and the church parsonage and school house were so damaged that nothing but the frames of the buildings were left standing. Windows, doors, siding, fences, seats from the church were either taken from the premises or destroyed."*[37]

Figure 9-Sanctuary, 1953

A two-year investigation enabled Congress to determine the Lewinsville community had voted to reject the bill of secession that had been passed in the state legislature. Two members who voted against secession, Mason Shipman and James Magarity, lived to testify at the 1903 hearing that approved the awarding of damages to Lewinsville Presbyterian Church. The Government paid $1,760 for damages in 1903, mostly to

---

[35] Ibid., *A Brief History*, p. 7
[36] Ibid.
[37] Ibid., *A Concise History*, p. 18, Testimony, US Court of Claims, 1903

24 || Pilgrims and Pioneers Always

reimburse the church for expenses incurred in 1866 to restore the church to "usable condition."[38]

During the three-year pastorate of Rev. Edward H. Bronson[39] (1904 - 1907), the congregation remodeled the interior of the church and a number of changes were made. The ceiling was lowered and electric lights installed. The oil-fueled pulpit lamp that had served pastors well for nearly half a century was turned over to the family of Hunter Mack.[40]

As for the walls, they decided to cover everything, including damaged plaster, with Philadelphia fencing. (Damaged plaster behind the fencing was discovered when the church was disassembled in 1956.) The fencing material was mounted as 36-inch wainscoting topped with chair rail. The remainder of the wall surface, from chair rail to ceiling, was covered with more of the natural oak fencing, installed on a diagonal and joined at the center of each wall. New curved pews were bought, and the slave balcony removed.[41] New carpeting was installed and two new pulpit chairs purchased. With funds left over, a metal shingle roof was laid. The physical appearance of the church did not change appreciably until 1955 when it was disassembled to make way for the new sanctuary.

Impact of Great Falls and Old Dominion Railroad

When railroads arrived in the area, the evolution of commerce was accelerated. In the early twentieth century, civic leaders understood that a railroad through your town—even if only a trolley line—was a prescription

---

[38] Ibid., p. 14
[39] Rev. Bronson was the only former pastor still living at the time of the 1946 Centennial Celebration. In 1946, Rev. Bronson was living in Upper Darby, Pennsylvania.
[40] Hunter Mack kept the lamp safe until his death. His wife, Alda, personally delivered the lamp to Rev. Franklin Gillespie before she died, and Gillespie return the lamp to Lewinsville in time for the 150th anniversary in 1996.
[41] Photos show 14 pews, arranged in two rows of seven, with a center aisle. Capacity ranged from 112 to 124, excluding the small choir. In one photo, a dozen additional folding chairs appear in the rear of the sanctuary.

for growth and success.

But it must have been amazing to watch the impact of a little technology on the lives of Lewinsville residents. In 1903, construction began on the Great Falls and Old Dominion Railroad, a suburban trolley line that ran through the heart of McLean, a total length of fourteen miles, connecting Georgetown with Great Falls. And it was electric! When the line opened in 1906, it became an instant success. People from Washington delighted in taking the trolley into the country "all the way to Great Falls." Some children even commuted to schools in Washington via the trolley.

For a while, the trolley made a stop for local residents on Ingleside Avenue. Residents finally decided to name the trolley stop in honor of John R. McLean, publisher of the Washington Post. McLean thrived, while the little communities of Langley and Lewinsville dried up.

Circuit Riders Keep Church Alive

Even as McLean was growing, attendance at Lewinsville remained fairly sparse. Services were conducted by a circuit rider, mostly on Sunday afternoons, because the circuit rider preached elsewhere on Sunday mornings. This was the custom of Rev. William R. McElroy who lived in Falls Church and conducted services at Lewinsville on Sunday afternoons between 1919 and 1923, and for Dr. J. Harvey Dunham who preached at Western Presbyterian Sunday mornings and served Lewinsville as Stated Supply on Sunday afternoons from 1923 to 1939.

Rev. McElroy was well known to the late Frances Hileman Kennedy, (1908-2007). She was a young girl when she began attending Sunday School and fourteen years of age in 1922 when she joined the church.[42] "Rev. McElroy always brought several of his sons along—he had six—and made them sit in the front pew so he could keep an eye on

---

[42] When Frances Kennedy died in 2007, she had been a member for eighty-five years. Without question, Frances Kennedy holds the record for longest serving member of Lewinsville.

them." Frances laughed. "I can't imagine a church I'd rather belong to than Lewinsville." [43]

**

---

[43] Kennedy Interview, *In the Spotlight*, church bulletin, March 1986.

Chapter Five
The Lean Years

Of the sixteen pastors who led Lewinsville through the twentieth century, three pastors played central roles in leading the church during pivotal moments of spiritual maturity and growth. Through their singular efforts at critical periods, Lewinsville was transformed from a struggling rural church in the 1920s to one of the stronger churches in the National Capital Presbytery by 2000. In this chapter, the roles of Dr. J. Harvey Dunham and Dr. Franklin B. Gillespie will be explored. The third pastor, Rev. Gary G. Pinder, who served from 1968 to 2005, will be described more fully in subsequent chapters. All three pastors played key roles in holding Lewinsville together through thick and thin (sometimes very thin), leading it forward in faith in times of great uncertainty, and trusting in Almighty God to show the way.

Dr. J. Harvey Dunham (1923-1939)

Dr. Dunham was Pastor of Western Presbyterian Church in Washington while serving as Stated Supply to Lewinsville from 1923 to 1939. Western, a thriving urban church in the heart of Washington, was the opposite of Lewinsville, a struggling rural church hardly anyone had ever heard of. When Dr. Dunham arrived for his first Sunday in the pulpit, he expected to preside that day over a congregational vote on the question of whether or not to continue regular services. Attendance had been sparse of late. But they never got around to a vote. In the middle of his sermon that Sunday afternoon in October, 1923, the stovepipe from the potbelly stove toppled over and baptized the entire congregation with black soot. The congregation of less than a score ran into the churchyard, coughing and sputtering. As they wiped soot from their faces, several among them expressed the view that the soot was God's way of telling them to stay. And so, they did. "Rather than be blinded by the soot," one of the elders later reported, "the Holy Spirit used the soot to open our eyes to a Lewinsville future known only to God."

Instead of closing the doors, the small congregation asked Dr. Dunham to continue as Stated Supply. He agreed. He never imagined he would serve in that capacity for nearly seventeen years.

From the beginning of Dr. Dunham's ministry, there was steady growth, and by 1927, membership was sixty-five with Sunday School registration on the rise as well. Many urban centers were experiencing an "outflow" of population in the 1920s and no one was more aware of that disruption in urban life than Dr. Dunham. Businesses and institutions were encroaching on suburban neighborhoods, and new homes were becoming an irresistible magnet for growing families.[44] Dr. Dunham was an eyewitness to the outward migration, and probably had mixed emotions as he watched his congregation at Western Presbyterian dwindle down while Lewinsville grew larger with each passing week. By the end of 1927, the need for new Sunday School facilities could no longer be ignored. Lewinsville needed larger classrooms and an auditorium where social events could be held.

Ground was broken in 1928 for a new multi-purpose educational building. At the dedication service, Elder J.C. Storm announced the building would be named in honor of Dr. J. Harvey Dunham, their beloved pastor who helped breathe new life into their church at a critical point in its ministry.[45]

In 1938, a two-manual Moller organ[46] was donated by the Clemens Storm family to replace the small reed organ that had served the

---

[44] Western Presbyterian Church history, www.westernchurch.net
[45] Dr. Dunham served Western Presbyterian and Lewinsville until his retirement in 1939.
[46] See **Appendix II** for history of the Lewinsville organs.

church for thirty years. Longtime member Juanita Shields became the first organist, "Because," she said, "no one else knew how to play it."[47] The reed organ was moved to Dunham Hall where it remained in service for many years. In addition to the pipe organ, a new oil heating system, drapes and flags were installed in the years leading up to Lewinsville's 1946 centennial celebration.

> *"The trolley line has had its day; now it's time for a car!"*
> **The railroad that had displaced Lewinsville as the center of commerce in the community was itself a victim of advances in transportation technology. The automobile, often ridiculed just twenty-five years before, had gained acceptance, and demand for it was growing. "The trolley line has had its day," one of the elders said. "Now it's time for a car!" The Great Falls trolley line discontinued operations in 1934, and the tracks were torn up to make way for a blacktop strip of pavement named Old Dominion Drive.**

When Dr. Dunham retired in 1939, the congregation of ninety members felt it was finally large enough to support a call to a full-time pastor. The conservative Scots-Irish leaders of the church concluded they could not afford an older, more seasoned pastor and began to look almost exclusively at young seminary graduates. This was a disappointment to Dr. Dunham who had anticipated becoming Lewinsville's full time pastor upon his retirement from Western Presbyterian Church.[48]

---

[47] Shields Interview, *In the Spotlight*, church bulletin, July 1986.
[48] Video Interview, Gapp, 1986

Rev. Franklin Brown Gillespie (1940-1948)

For weeks, church members took turns travelling to Union Station to pick up candidates from Princeton Seminary and bring them to Lewinsville to preach the Sunday message. After almost a year of interviews and listening to sermons, the congregation settled on a newly minted graduate from Princeton, Franklin Brown Gillespie. Rev. Gillespie arrived May 15, 1940, with his fiancée Marion Weiss by his side. Their car was loaded with all their worldly possessions.

The trip from Princeton to Lewinsville led to an inauspicious beginning for the new pastor. A congregational dinner was scheduled for four o'clock, followed by the installation service at eight o'clock. Rev. Gillespie allowed plenty of time for the trip but did not count on his car breaking down. Unfortunately, he was forced to stop for repairs several times. Through the afternoon, his clothes became progressively dirtier with oil and grease. Finally, he called the church to alert the elders of his predicament. "I'll be late," he said, "uh, by about four hours—but I *will* be there." At 8:15 p.m., they started the service without him. When he arrived, someone threw a robe over his oily clothes and he rushed onto the platform but not before his fiancé wiped a large oil splotch from his forehead. "Fortunately, my part was not until the benediction but as I sat there, I realized I reeked of oil and gasoline. I also realized the presiding pastor had begun by reading the opening of a funeral service, not an installation service." His eyes twinkled as he looked at the interviewer. "What have I gotten myself into?"[49]

---

[49] Video Interview, Gillespie, October 19, 1986

A Period of Great Transition

Years later, Rev. Gillespie returned to deliver the celebration sermon for the 140th anniversary. He recalled the 1940s as a period of great transition for the church, from a strictly rural church to a suburban church, surrounded by a developing community. "We had a strong Sunday School, a fine choir, a good organ, and a good organist," Gillespie recalled. "But church finances were not so hot. The Ladies Aid Society carried the church through many a difficult financial patch. When funds were needed, the Ladies Aid Society put on a dinner. Everybody came because they were known throughout the community for their culinary skills. They had no difficulty in raising funds when required."[50]

Figure 10-Ladies Aid Leadership, 1946

He praised the church of the early 1940s for its many strong attributes but there was one weakness. "I must say I also found a self-centered congregation." He explained that the pledge card in use at the time was divided into two sides, one for expenses and the other for benevolences. "The church gave $80 annually to benevolences—$75 to local charities and $5 allocated alternately each year between the Board of Foreign Missions and the Board of National Missions." To his dismay, he found that church leaders were assigning all funds, regardless of which side of the card was specified, to expenses of the church. "I put a stop to that."[51]

> *"...this starry-eyed young dreamer."*

---

[50] Sermon by Gillespie, 140th anniversary of Lewinsville Presbyterian Church, October 19, 1986
[51] Ibid.

Rev. Gillespie proposed a budget of $3,200 for 1941, with 10 percent set aside for benevolences. Members of the search committee, he was sure, were wondering if they made a mistake in calling "this starry-eyed young dreamer."[52]

Figure 11-Entire Sunday School gathered outside Dunham Hall in the late 1940's

By 1945, the Sunday School program had completely out grown Dunham Hall. The building that, at its dedication in 1929, was praised for its potential to meet the church's needs for perhaps 100 years was now completely inadequate for the growing education program. Rather than expand Dunham Hall outward on existing property, the congregation decided it would be less expensive to lift the building by the height of a full basement and put classrooms underneath. When they were finished, this improvement provided seven new class rooms, two rest rooms, and an oil burning hot water heating system. While they were making improvements, they enlarged the kitchen and replaced all kitchen equipment.

The classroom area in the expanded building was named, The Frech Memorial, in honor of longtime Sunday School superintendent J.P. Frech, who served from 1926 to 1942. "There was no one to whom the children of the Sunday School meant as much as this man," wrote Rev. Gillespie in his history of Lewinsville. "His primary aim was to teach the boys and girls the Christian truths of the Bible, which he so well lived

---

[52] Rev. Gillespie was offered a starting salary of $1,800 per year in 1940

out in his own life."[53] The Frech Memorial was dedicated in 1946 as part of the Centennial Celebration. With the expansion complete, Dunham Hall was now of a sufficient size to meet the educational needs of Lewinsville—they hoped—for fifteen or twenty years. A lot of fingers were crossed.

Figure 12-Original Manse, built 1830

The Manse, built in 1830, was seldom used as a manse since the pulpit was occupied frequently by circuit riders or Stated Supplies. In the late 1940s, it was purchased by Bayard Evans, moved a short distance to his property next door, and completely restored. For many years, the renovated Manse next door was the home of member J. Carlton Van Wagoner.

A new Manse was erected on church property in the late 1940s, and is now in use as The Pastoral Counseling and Consultation Centers of Greater Washington.[54]

Church membership grew from about 100 members in 1940 to 189 in 1946. By 1947, the veterans of World War II had come home, and the Baby Boomer generation was just getting started. Families were arriving in Northern Virginia in large numbers. From the end of the decade until well into the 1960s, almost all protestant churches grew. Lewinsville was no exception.

Figure 13-Second Manse, built 1940's, now Pastoral Counseling Center

---

[53] Ibid., *A Brief History*, p.25
[54] This facility provides ecumenical, mental health counseling. In addition to clinical work, the Centers also engage in education work with psychotherapists from various disciplines, family therapists, lay persons, and married couples.

1952 Friendship Quilt

The best evidence of the growth experienced immediately after the war is found in the 1952 Friendship Quilt which the Ladies Aid Society made to commemorate the 100-year span of time since the crafting of their first quilt. Altogether, 411 names are honored on it.

The quilt, approximately fifty-six square feet, is displayed in the stairwell connecting St. Andrews Hall on the main level and Fellowship Hall in the basement. A conscientious effort was made to include the names of every family and family member on the official church roll in 1952.

The tradition of quilting established in 1852 and demonstrated again in 1952 is carried on today by another quilting group—Lost Sheep Stitchers. Their mission is to provide prayer shawls and afghans to home-bound members and those in nursing homes with the goal of expressing the love, concern and appreciation of a grateful congregation. And beyond that mission, they are supporting efforts to assist wounded warriors, children in crisis and persons in hospice care. "If it involves needles, we will do it," Nancy McGuire said.

During the twenty-year transitional period between Rev. Gillespie and Rev. Pinder, three pastors played significant roles in laying a foundation for future success. It was a period of frenetic change, to be sure, but Lewinsville was fortunate that the responsibility for those years fell to Rev. James Lundquist (1948-1953), Dr. Howard Newman (1954-1957), and Rev. John Graham (1957-1969).

✶✶

Chapter Six
End of an Era, Beginning of Another

In 1947, the church was growing rapidly as brand new post-war automobiles brought families, anxious to escape the city, to the suburbs. Everyone at Lewinsville was busy trying to meet the challenge of rapid growth. The next dozen years ushered in a new age that dramatically changed the world and reshaped established institutions. Most people did not recognize the significance of the changes at the time.

Hardly anyone took notice, for example, when engineers at Bell Labs invented the transistor in 1947, but that single step forward became the fundamental building block for all the computers and telephones the world depends upon today.

Early television receivers were using vacuum tubes, not transistors, to bring television programs into America's homes. Most TV programs consisted of images that were often "snowy" and "ghostly" in appearance, but what an impact the proliferation of television sets made on our society. Some have said The Ed Sullivan Variety Show single-handedly canceled Sunday night worship services where they were being held. And when Elvis Presley made his first appearance on the show in September 1956 to the largest audience in television history at that time, the medium's place in American culture was secured. Of course, the entertainment world also was changed forever.

When the *Brown v. Board of Education* decision was handed down by the Supreme Court in 1954, the segregated world as it existed in America was suddenly on its last legs. The fight for the civil rights of all Americans officially began that day—and in many ways, continues.

In 1958, the Russians launched their Sputnik satellite, and the space race was on in earnest. Educational institutions were asked to improve math and science curricula in order to produce enough scientists and engineers to enable America to compete with the Russians.

We often look back to the 1950s as a "Donna Reed time in America." America was happy with its "baseball, hot dogs, and apple pie" world. Dwight Eisenhower was President for most of those years, and despite the Korean conflict and periodic outburst of unrest overseas, the Baby Boomers were growing up in a relatively stable world. They wished it would stay that way, but underneath that checkered-apron world, everything was changing.

Figure 14-Officers of the church gather at entrance for group photo in late 1940s

Churches had little time in the 1950s to examine the fundamental changes taking place in American society. They were growing! Neighborhoods were thriving. New schools and new churches were being built to accommodate the growth.

Besides, many pastors thought some of these modern things, like television, were just a passing fad and would die out just as Rev. C.B. McKee hoped in 1852 that the notion of women leading prayer would "die out." Or, maybe not.

Rev. James Lundquist (1948-1953)

Rev. Jim Lundquist arrived at Lewinsville in 1948 when the congregation had surged past two hundred members. Very soon, two services on Sunday morning were required to accommodate the growing numbers. Parking around the circular driveway was already at a premium, and inside, pews were full to overflowing. Dunham Hall was bursting at the seams. To relieve crowding, the pastor had to make the parlor of the manse available every Sunday for an adult class.

Photos taken before Rev. Lundquist arrived reveal the sanctuary as it appeared nearly unchanged since the 1908 renovation and repairs. The brass cross on the communion table in photo was a 1945 gift from Mrs. Grace M. Clarke.

Figure 15-Sanctuary, 1946

The cross welcomes visitors to the church office today.

The silk Christian and United States flags in photo above were gifts from Mrs. Archer Haycock, and were dedicated Palm Sunday, April 14, 1946.

The sanctuary featured seven rows of pews on either side of a center aisle. The photo below reveals a small vestibule and about a dozen chairs brought in to handle overflow.

The final worship service in the old church took place on November 27, 1955.

Lewinsville was no longer that little country church "out there" in the woods near McLean, Virginia.

Dr. Howard F. Newman (1954-1957)

A committee had already completed two years of work on plans for a new sanctuary when Dr. Howard Newman arrived in 1954. Membership was recorded at 547 and growing. Dr. Newman wasted no time in urging Session to finish its plans for a new sanctuary. As much as the congregation wanted to find a way to integrate the original structure into the new sanctuary, its fate was sealed when they discovered it riddled with termites and in real danger of falling down. It was not even strong enough to survive a gentle move to a small corner of the property. On December 17, 1955, the last features of the wood frame structure were removed, but not before some of its timbers were saved by Dr. Newman for a future undesignated use.[55] For six months, the congregation met in the McLean High School auditorium while the original church was disassembled and construction begun on a new sanctuary for Lewinsville.

On May 6, 1956, a stone from the original church was laid and dedicated as the cornerstone for the new sanctuary. Elder J. Clemons Storm laid the cornerstone.[56] The trowel he used that day is retained in

---

[55] When a cross was installed on the lawn of the present day church in the early 1980s, it was crafted entirely from two support beams that survived the original church. Even these beams succumbed to weather and insects by 2010. Small pieces of wood trim from the original cross were used on the new (metal) cross installed and dedicated May 2010.
[56] The Storm family was active for many decades in church life and donated the second reed organ to the church in 1938.

Lewinsville archives. Dr. Howard Newman conducted the service. Frank Gapp, church historian, described the stone's history. Unfortunately, a text of remarks delivered cannot be found.

Figure 16- (Left to right) J. Clemons Storm, Dr. Howard Newman, Frank Gapp

In December 1955,
the old church was
carefully and lovingly
disassembled to make way for a
new and larger sanctuary.

Construction of the new sanctuary began in early 1956.

The congregation of 1956 remained true to the "meeting house" architectural style of the first church. The primary difference: the sanctuary was large enough to accommodate 340 in the pews.[57]

Lewinsville was not the only institution feeling the effects of the post-war generation. Schools were adding classrooms, and churches were expanding as fast as they could. "Expansion" was the word on all lips when Rev. John Graham answered the call to come to Lewinsville.

Rev. John Graham (1957-1969)

The transformation of the little community surrounding Lewinsville was fully underway by the time Rev. John Graham arrived in May 1957. He was another freshly minted pastor, a recent graduate of the Theological Seminary of the University of Dubuque, Iowa, but he was definitely not a Midwestern native. Graham, a citizen of the United Kingdom, was a gunner for the Royal Air Force during World War II. After the war, he found his way to the States where he made a decision to enter the ministry. When Graham arrived at Lewinsville, he had little or no previous full-time training. What he lacked in experience, however, he more than made up in youthful energy.

Rev. Graham recruited Miss Yvonne Greatwood in 1958 as Director of Christian Education—a volunteer position—and launched an effort to replace Dunham Hall, which had served the church well for thirty-five years. The new education facility was named Heritage Hall when dedicated in 1962. The total construction cost of Heritage Hall was $167,000.

---

[57] See **Appendix III** for a detailed physical description of the 1956 church as contained in the dedication program

Long-time member J. Clemons Stone, age seventy-eight in photo above, with hand on cornerstone of the new education building in 1961.

In lower left photo, progress in the construction of Heritage Hall was captured from the high grass across Chain Bridge Road.

Figure 17-Dunham Hall while still in use. Note classrooms on basement level that were added in 1945.

"In two years, the building was planned, funds were raised, and construction completed," Rev. Graham reported.[58] In other words, there was no mortgage to be paid, and that is a tradition the church has maintained each time a new capital project has been proposed through the years.

Dunham Hall was eventually sold for $1 to Ralph Evans and moved to Evans Farm Inn adjacent to Lewinsville. Evans, a Lewinsville member, converted Dunham Hall into a gift/antique shop for his "farmette" of sixteen acres and restaurant.

Figure 18-Dunham Hall rolling to Evans Farm

"...from a rural church to a suburban church located smack in the middle of one of the fastest growing counties in America."

---

[58] Annual Report of the Pastor, as it appeared in the Dedication Program, February 18, 1962

The little church which previously attracted most of its members from dairy farms and small local businesses suddenly found itself home to hundreds of government bureaucrats from all three branches of the Federal Government. Members of Congress and their aides, CIA personnel, employees of think tanks, experts from a full alphabet soup of federal agencies, bureaucrats from the Census Bureau, State Department, Defense, and HEW (now HHS), to name a few, filled the pews.

Figure 19-Rev. Graham, 1986

"We were changing from a rural church to a suburban church located smack in the middle of one of the fastest growing counties in America," Rev. Graham recalled in 1986. "I remember with pride our willingness to adapt as a church to serve the local community. We had been inward focused and satisfied with things the way they were. But that changed when the congregation took a first option on the Hammond/Eglin property next door to the church."[59]

**

---

[59] Video Interview, Graham, October 19, 1986

Chapter Seven
Beyond These Walls

Many members of the congregation look back to July 12, 1967, the day the decision was made to purchase the Hammond/Eglin property, as the first day of the modern Lewinsville Presbyterian Church. It has been described as the day Lewinsville began to spread its wings of faith beyond its walls.

By a unanimous vote, the congregation agreed to pay $91,213 for 3.86 acres next door—the Hammond/Eglin property—with no idea of its use beyond the belief that God would lead the church to his purpose for it. "It is impossible to predict exactly what use will be made of the property, in particular, or as a whole. But one thing is sure, without additional land it will be impossible for ourselves or those who follow us to minister to the spiritual needs of the rapidly growing community."[60] That single leap of faith in 1967 opened a wide door to the pursuit of mission outreach programs stretching from Lewinsville's backyard to the highest mountains of Nepal.

---

[60] Brochure language prepared to explain all relevant facts surrounding the purchase of the land, 1967

Rev. Gary George Pinder (1968-2005)

In the midst of all the change taking place in the world and at Lewinsville in the late 1960s, a young man from Rochester, New York, was called to Lewinsville to serve as Associate Pastor with Rev. John Graham.

Rev. Pinder was a graduate of the College of Wooster and Pittsburgh Theological Seminary. In 1965, he was ordained by the Westminster Presbyterian Church of Dayton, Ohio. He was installed at Lewinsville in October 1968, as Associate Pastor, with an emphasis on adult and youth education. When Rev. Graham left less than year later, the Book of Order did not permit Rev. Pinder to assume the duties of Pastor, and the Presbyterian Church had no "interim pastor" position at that time. The pulpit was declared vacant and the Rev. Carl Cooper of nearby Immanuel Presbyterian Church was appointed moderator of Lewinsville's Session. The pulpit may have been "vacant" by official declaration, but it was filled admirably by Rev. Pinder while the church waited for the next pastor to be called. Pinder was the only pastor in Lewinsville's history to hold the titles of Associate Pastor, Co-Pastor, and finally Senior Pastor. When he retired the congregation voted to give him yet another title: Pastor Emeritus. The story of those changes in his title along the way is the story of Lewinsville Presbyterian Church in modern times.

"...where do we go from here?"

At retirement in 2005, Rev. Pinder was the longest serving ordained pastor in Lewinsville's history, and the contribution he made to every aspect of the congregation's life in his thirty-seven years enabled the church to enter the twenty-first century as an active, vibrant church, working to achieve its full potential. But this is not a story about Rev. Pinder. He would rather it be a story about the people of Lewinsville and how they responded to their faith, and so it is. But Rev. Pinder's role for thirty-seven years was integral to the congregation's success. He was constantly asking the question: "Where do we go from here?" Human nature is resistant to change, and there are always many who prefer the status quo. But change was in the air, and Rev. Pinder kept Lewinsville prepared to embrace it.

> ***"...the time has come to make change an ally..."***

Rev. William J. Tatum (1971-1977)

In Rev. William J. Tatum, Gary Pinder found a colleague ready to join him in meeting the challenges presented by the 1970s. "There is no way to prevent change," Tatum wrote to the congregation, "nor should we if we could. For in this swiftly changing world, the Gospel most needs to be presented in the present context. Frankly, the time has come to make change an ally rather than an enemy."[61] But then he added something worthy of remembering by each succeeding generation. "Above all, there is the call to renewal in this age. To be a disciple of Jesus Christ is to be disciplined by him. This is not only a personal commitment, but if we take the New Testament seriously, it is a commitment to the fellowship of faith, too."[62]

---

[61] Pastor's letter to congregation, June 1972
[62] Ibid.

> The late 1960s and early 1970s were a period of great social turmoil in America. The nation was split over support for the Vietnam War. Nowhere was the discord felt more keenly than among the members of Lewinsville, many of whom came from leadership positions in government and represented the full range of political interests. Hal Saunders, member and State Department senior diplomat in the Arab-Israeli peace process, worked with Rev. Pinder to plan a three evening lecture series in April 1971, titled, "Christians Reflect on War." The series, a resounding success, was the forerunner of many public policy discussions at Lewinsville that ultimately led to establishing the Faith and Public Policy Breakfasts series in 2003. Generally, these breakfast discussions number three or four each year, and there has never been a shortage of topics.

Rev. Tatum was installed September 12, 1971. Under the leadership of both pastors, Tatum and Pinder, Lewinsville soon completed the difficult task of transitioning to a unicameral form of governance, incorporating trustees and deacons with the Session. It proved unwieldy from the start but the pastors soldiered on undaunted, even when Session meetings lasted into the early morning. (More about this experiment later.) The unicameral Session had some big ideas, one of which was the concept of finding a way to extend the mission ministry of the church into the community.

In September 1973, Session made the Eglin property next door available for the use of Alternative House. Soon, it was providing critically needed assistance to runaways seeking shelter and counseling. Even as Alternative House took advantage of the property, Session knew long-range planning was needed to discover its best use. The first strategic planning committee Session formed became deadlocked over whether to build a new sanctuary or some type of community facility. Unable to make a decision, they reported their stalemate to Session which immediately dissolved the committee and formed another. With a more diverse range of interests represented on the committee, the members developed a long list of options for Session to consider, but at the top of that list was "housing for the elderly."

Lewinsville Retirement Residence is Born

A couple of years of further discussion ensued before the Session decided that affordable housing for senior citizens was the one most unmet need existing in the rapidly growing McLean community. In 1975, the church established a legally separate, non-profit, corporation to turn this vision into a reality.

In the midst of planning and designing the new affordable living facility, the church confronted the untimely resignation of Rev. Tatum in 1977. A serious illness had forced his resignation.

And now there was another problem.

A Co-Pastorate is Created

The congregation had grown quite fond of Rev. Pinder and wanted to elevate him to Pastor. The rules of the Presbyterian Church, however, did not permit an Associate Pastor to be promoted to Pastor in the same church he was serving. The only path open to the congregation was to create a co-pastorate and give both pastors the title. The rules permitted co-pastors to be promoted to Pastor and that was the *only* path that could possibly lead Rev. Pinder to the position of Pastor in the future. That was enough to satisfy the interests of all parties. The co-pastorate was created by the congregation on September 25, 1977. Both pastors accepted the new title.

> *"Many members did not know what a co-pastorate was…"*

Rev. John Preston Smith (1979-1985)

Rev. John Smith was called in September 1979 to join Rev. Pinder. They served as co-pastors for a while, but in the end, it did not work out.

"Many members did not know what a co-pastorate was," Rev. Smith recalled. "We learned how it worked together. It was somewhat difficult for Session. They wondered who was in charge…but I think it answered the needs of the congregation at that time."[63]

When Rev. Smith resigned in 1985, Rev. Pinder was made Senior Pastor, a position he held for twenty years. In retrospect, it is easier to see that Rev. Pinder was, indeed, the essential constant in the life of the church almost from the day he arrived. He stepped in to lead when John Graham left. He was ready when Bill Tatum fell ill. He became the captain at the tiller who stilled the waters in rough seas and the inspiration that sailed the church forward with "a full sheet," always with one steady hand on the helm and the other on the Bible.

Marie T. Lewis

Never was that steady hand needed more than when the church was trying to navigate the uncharted territory of building a retirement residence for the elderly. Fortunately, bringing The Lewinsville Retirement Residence to fruition was a passion for Marie T. Lewis. She enthusiastically assumed leadership of the project and served as first president of the board of directors of LRR, Inc.

Role models in Christian discipleship are not hard to find in Lewinsville's history. Marie Lewis was one of those, a gentle but

---

[63] Video Interview, Smith, October 19, 1986

resolute woman whose tenacious application of personal energy and charm built Lewinsville Retirement Residence. There can be no question about it, without Marie Lewis, The Lewinsville Residence would not exist today. The record of her accomplishment is well documented.

> *"...What if we build this facility and we can't fill it up?"*

Funding for the new residence was arranged through a $5.3 million loan from the Department of Housing and Urban Development. A few days before the loan documents were scheduled to be signed, a member of Marie's board of directors asked a final question, "But what if we build this facility and we can't fill it up. We, that is, Lewinsville Church will still be on the hook for the entire monthly mortgage payment." It sounded ominous, and the room was quiet for a few minutes. Finally, Marie Lewis said, "In a church, you're supposed to do some things on faith. Nothing is certain, of course, but God has led us successfully thus far. Shouldn't our faith be strong enough to see this project through?" All were quiet.

Figure 20-Groundbreaking for LRR, 1979

Another member of the group spoke up. "You'd never make a decision this way in a business."

"This is *not* a business," Marie Lewis said, in a determined voice. "This is a church, and we have, in case you haven't noticed, a very strong partner."[64]

---

[64] Author's personal recollection of a 1978 conversation among LRR board members

> "She made it come together..."
> While many have played key roles in the success of The Lewinsville over the years, there is one person whose passion for the project never wavered and whose indefatigable efforts overcame every obstacle: Marie Lewis.
> Rev. William J. Tatum, pastor during the germination years for The Lewinsville Retirement Residence, returned for the 140th church anniversary and praised Marie Lewis for her grace and persistence with the project. "The thing I remember most fondly from my years at Lewinsville is all the effort—all the leadership—and how it came together in that wonderful chairperson, Marie Lewis," Tatum said. "This was the first project HUD approved under its 202 program, so it presented many hurdles. She made it come together in spite of all the obstacles encountered, and it became a model for similar projects nationwide."

Two days later, the HUD agreement was signed, and the commitment made by the LRR board of directors on behalf of Lewinsville Church. It is important to note that all Lewinsville members are automatically members of the corporation that owns and operates the Lewinsville Retirement Residence. And only members of the church are eligible to serve on its board of directors.

Under the terms of the loan, the church was paid $165,000 for the property, not a bad return on its ten-year investment. Ground was broken May 6, 1979, and The Lewinsville opened September 29, 1980, with a long waiting list.

Figure 21-Lewinsville Retirement Residence

The Lewinsville's 144 apartment units are home to 150 residents, ages sixty to over 100. The majority of the residents receive a rental subsidy, but often those subsidies are not enough.

To meet their needs, Friends of the Lewinsville was formed to provide a Resident Services Program. Through the Friends program and the Caring Hands Endowment Fund created by members of the church, meal assistance and a number of other personal services are provided.

Music at Lewinsville

Members can be forgiven if they think Lewinsville did not have a music program prior to the arrival of J. Clark in 1967. He was a brilliant organist, an inspired conductor and leader of choirs, and a gifted composer, but he was also building every day on a legacy begun by many others.

In the 1850s, there was no organ, just the congregation singing *a cappella*, led by Mrs. Suzanna Storm. When the first reed organ was installed in the 1870s, the organist was Miss Nellie Hunter, and later, Miss Annie Mankin, both Lewinsville members. Miss Mankin played the organ for thirty years before she and the organ retired. A second reed organ was installed in 1908, and it also served thirty years. In 1938, the congregation had no choice but to accept its totally exhausted condition. Repairs could no longer be made cost effectively. The Storm family stepped up with a donation that brought a two-manual Moller organ to Lewinsville. No one knew how to play it so another volunteer, Juanita Shields, stepped forward. When Juanita took over, she began a tradition of excellence in Lewinsville music that continues today.[65]

---

[65] See **Appendix II** for history of Lewinsville's organs

J. Franklin Clark

J. Clark, Organist and Choir Director, arrived in July 1967, a year before Rev. Pinder. He received his undergraduate degree from Evansville College and a Master's degree from New England Conservatory of Music. He also attended the Episcopal Theological School in Cambridge, Massachusetts.

J. Clark began his ministry playing the old 1938 Moller organ but let it be known he was not happy with it. The Moller was replaced a year later with a Casavant organ. It served the church well until 1985 when it was replaced by an instrument built by the Gress-Miles Pipe Organ Company of Princeton, New Jersey. The organ was a gift to Lewinsville from Roy and Nancy Mitchell.

By the time J. retired, the record of his ministry at Lewinsville was known throughout the country. At one time, 160 persons were participating in eleven choral and handbell choirs, spanning ages from pre-school to adult. The youth choirs often performed original works by Pamela Lawson, Ethelmae Page and J. Clark while on tours in the eastern United States.[66]

J. came to Lewinsville with the title, Organist-Choir Director, but at his request, it was soon changed to Minister of Music, a more descriptive title, he said, for the ministry he was asked to undertake. "My job was more than making music; it was to bond choirs into a fellowship, to minister to the congregation, and to offer 100 percent of musical excellence every Sunday morning," he said. "We do not perform; we offer musical gifts."[67]

---

[66] See the **Appendix V** for a complete list of musical productions performed under the leadership of J. Clark.
[67] Minerva W. Andrews and Marian J. O'Brien, *The Church at Lewinsville at Millennium's Close*, 2002, p. 16

Several times a year, choirs performed with orchestra and also presented cantatas as fully staged productions in worship services. In the 1980s, Martha Britt assisted J. as substitute organist. She also took part in performances of choir, organ and orchestra. By 2000, J. was assisted by Judi Belzer, director of children's choirs; Frances Vaughn, director of youth handbells; Carole Huston, assistant organist; and four section leaders in the Chancel Choir. It is important to note that Carole Huston has been the steady metronome in Lewinsville's music program, a talented musician who has been called upon many times, especially in the uncertain time between leaders in the music program, to assure that continuity in musical excellence was maintained.

Figure 22-Carole Huston

The music complex was enlarged during the 1989 building project to include two rooms for rehearsing, another for robing, a library, and an office. Anna (Ann) Shaw stepped in and took charge of organizing the music library, and with the assistance of other volunteers, entered data to cross-reference 800 single anthems, 1,000 cantatas, 500 handbell pieces, and an assorted collection of anthems.

Expansion and Renovation begun in 1989

Figure 23-Groundbreaking, June 1989

Membership was well above 850 in the mid-1980s, generally ranging from 860 to 880. Attendance was high at both services on Sundays. At Easter and Christmas, worship services were full to overflowing, often requiring folding chairs to be added at the end of each pew, much to the consternation of the Fire Department. Elders serving Communion were often forced to sit in chairs placed against the wall on opposite sides of the chancel and suffer an obstructed view of the entire service.

The 1990 building project was the most ambitious and expensive project undertaken by Lewinsville on its current campus.

Financial Crisis Averted

From the start, the congregation knew the planned construction would require a major fundraising effort. Some 300 families pledged over $1.3 million, but as with many major projects of this nature and size, unexpected costs were encountered.

Figure 24-Construction, 1990

As work began on the sanctuary, the contractor discovered an asbestos problem in the ceiling. Remediation would be expensive but it could not be avoided. Estimates for the entire project soared to around $1.8 million. When the construction loan came due, the congregation lacked the total funds needed. An austerity operating budget for the following year was discussed, but before any action could be taken, Providence stepped in. Word was received that a

Figure 25-Construction in Sanctuary, pews removed

former member, Raymond Corbin, left an unsolicited gift of $250,000 to Lewinsville Church in his will. In addition, several members of the church made additional gifts totaling $125,000. The remaining deficit was erased with a temporary loan from the cemetery fund, and the financial crisis was averted.

> **"*The Barnacled Beavers*"**
> **John Calvin first described work as a calling from God. Maybe that's why followers of the Reformed Tradition are so quick to seize the work before them and just do it. If so, that explains how The Barnacled Beavers came into existence. A group of volunteers, led by Chuck Scheffey, organized themselves into a working group during the renovation of the sanctuary and construction of additions to the church campus and devoted their time to taking care of the ancillary things related to the project. The work was there and they just did it. The Beavers worked on the Sanctuary, the Narthex, the worship support area behind the Chancel, the administrative suite, Heritage Hall, the old Manse, landscaping, and the Memorial Garden. Twelve men, the youngest no more than sixty years of age, spent their Wednesdays, and a few other days of the week unaccounted for, and completed nearly sixty projects over three years. They were dedicated to the belief that work should not be for oneself, but for others. Every church should be so fortunate as to have a group of Barnacled Beavers among its membership.**

The entire project was finished and dedicated, October 1990. In addition to a sanctuary renovation, the church added a large narthex, elevator, and a separate music department. The breezeway and patio area between Heritage Hall and the Sanctuary were enclosed (and later renamed, St. Andrews Hall).

Lewinsville East

Commercial developers who sought to build a community of townhouses in 2003 on the adjacent Evans Farm Inn property made a gift of a small portion of their land to LRR, Inc., before their project moved forward. With great excitement, the board of LRR began searching for a source of funding while other members of the board worked on architectural plans for expansion.

Figure 26-Lewinsville East

Thanks to the vision and leadership of members William Chenault, President of LRR, Inc., and Sam Condit, LRR Building Committee Chair, HUD approved use of LRR's Reserve Fund (approximately $4 million accumulated over twenty years) to construct a new 18-unit building. The new building, known as "Lewinsville East," provides apartments for low and moderate income seniors. All are subsidized by the Fairfax County Affordable Dwelling Unit Program.

Figure 27-Peters' Property adjoins the church

Four years later, LRR and Lewinsville Church bought the remaining small particle of land situated between the church and the former Evans Farm property. It was just a small sliver of land, less than a full acre, but it connected Chain Bridge Road to The Lewinsville Retirement Residence property. Today, it is commonly referred to as "Peters' Green," because it was part of the estate of Katharine Peters who lived on the parcel until her death. When the sale was consummated in February 2007, the church had finally secured all land bordering the Evans Farm neighborhood. The purchase price was $1 million, a large sum, but it provided the church and LRR valuable space to fulfill a future vision. A specific use for the property still awaits a determination by the leadership of both organizations.

Roots of Lewinsville's Annual Summer Mission Project

Today, more than fifty youth and adults participate annually in Lewinsville's Summer Mission Project, an annual trek by car, truck and sometimes, plane, to help a brother or sister in need. For more than thirty years, they have traveled from Louisiana to New York and South Dakota, with hammers in hand and faith to fix up, clean up, and lift up those in need.

But the roots of this most successful mission endeavor began modestly in 1980 when Rev. Gary Pinder and his wife, Barbara, packed fifteen youth into two cars, and accompanied by four other adults, drove

1,500 miles to the Pine Ridge Indian Reservation (Oglala Sioux Tribe) Pine Ridge, South Dakota for a two-week work experience.[68] In recalling the trip west, Rev. Pinder said, "We

---

[68] Participants: Adults – Gary and Barbara Pinder, Tom Stedman, Ed Harmes and Martha Kreiger. Youth – Cindy Brownlee, Mary Kathleen Daugherty, David Dokken, Nancy Getreu, Cliff Hendrix, Carlie Masters, Marcia Miller, Suzy Miller, John Palmer, Rob Robertson, Melanie Smith, Thad Smith, Connie VanBrunt, Jane Wimbish, and Debbie Zanfagna.

used about as much oil in that Dodge maxi-van as we did gasoline, but no one complained."[69] Their assignment was to convert an old house into an educational building for the Oglala Sioux Tribe.

The youth found it to be a most meaningful experience, and for some, even life changing. When another trip did not automatically occur the next year, parents heard the disappointment of their children and encouraged Rev. Pinder to help organize a similar trip for the following summer.

> *"...the work will be hard, hot, and you will be dirty...but it will be the most rewarding experience..."*

Linda Bender has been a youth participant and adult organizer of the trip for more than twenty years. "These trips are not vacations," Linda emphasizes to the youth. "You will learn construction techniques and how to use tools properly. The work will be hard, hot, and you will be dirty eight hours a day, every day—and it will be the most rewarding experience of your life."[70]

Figure 28-Summer Mission Project 2013 traveled to the New Jersey shore to help with Hurricane Sandy recovery

Today, approximately fifty members adopt a Summer Mission Project somewhere in the United States, typically in an area that has suffered a natural disaster. In view of the SMP success, Linda Bender

---

[69] Video Interview, October 19, 1986, 140th anniversary
[70] See **Appendix VII** for list of Summer Mission Projects (1990-2013).

organized the first Winter Mission Project in January 2006.[71] These trips have also been enormously successful in spite of the sometimes frosty working conditions.

100 Mission Programs

The record today shows the church is intimately involved in nearly 100 external mission projects, including the support of eight missionaries around the globe. The Mission and Service Ministry Group is organized around four central areas of emphasis: Housing, Hunger and Poverty, Social Services, National and International.

Housing Mission Activities
- Chesterbrook Residences
- Hearts & Hammers
- Homestretch
- Lewinsville Retirement Residence
- McLean Interfaith Coalition
- Rebuilding Together
- Summer Mission Project

Hunger and Poverty Activities
- Christ House
- Miriam's Kitchen
- SHARE
- United Health Care

Social Services Activities
- Falls Church-McLean Children's Center
- Alternative house
- Bethany House of Northern Virginia
- Good News Jail & Prison Ministry
- L'Arche of Greater Washington, DC
- Children of Mine Center
- Ingleside Presbyterian Retirement Community

National and International Activities
- Basic Mission Support
- Elburgon Presbytery in Kenya
- Soymilk for North Korean Orphans
- Papua New Guinea Bible and Medical Mission
- Holy Land Christian Ecumenical Foundation
- Poor Children's Assistance Project
- Disaster Relief
- Boost the Troops
- Partners for Just Trade

---

[71] Linda Bender also has served as Interim Youth Director four times: 2001, 2003, 2005 and 2008 and as a member of Session on three separate occasions.

Basic mission support is also provided to:
- Frank and Nancy Dimmock, Lesotho
- Andrew and Ellen Collins, Chiang Mai, Thailand
- Art and Sue Kinsler, Seoul, South Korea
- Brian and Helen Chapaitis, Papua New Guinea

Figure 29-Helen Chapaitis

Lewinsville has clearly come a long way from struggling to stay alive and meet its meager budget year to year. Gone are the days when the church set aside $80 annually for "benevolence" purposes, then spent those funds on ordinary expenses.

"Today's congregation is committed to mission giving through financial pledges, emergency appeals, hands-on work, food and household collection drives, fair trade support, as well as support for mission co-workers," said Associate Pastor, Emily Berman D'Andrea. "And there is a greater awareness of the joy that comes from serving our neighbor."

Somewhere in a storeroom of Lewinsville Church, an old poster is tucked away that reads, "The World Is My Neighbor, It Shall Not Want." The poster is no longer gracing a wall but the words are certainly being lived out by the congregation.

Figure 30-Aerial view in the mid-1980s reveals the entire complex; the Sanctuary, Heritage Hall, the Old Manse, and the Lewinsville Retirement Residence

**

Chapter Eight
Christian Formation

In the era of volunteer Yvonne Greatwood, Lewinsville's first Director of Christian Education (1958-1961), teachers focused almost exclusively on Bible Study and memorization of the Child's Catechism. Ms. Greatwood once had a student recite the entire book of John. Some of her high school students even mastered the Westminster Shorter Catechism. Members of a certain age will always remember the answer to its first question: "What is man's chief end?"[72]

Constantly Evolving

Yvonne Greatwood was, of course, an unpaid volunteer. Resources were scarce, and church school education depended on volunteers. Instead of a CE Coordinator, Lewinsville, like most Presbyterian churches of the time, relied on the leadership of a Superintendent.

> *"…there are no thankless jobs when one is serving the Lord…"*

If J.P. Frech, Lewinsville's beloved Sunday School Superintendent in the 1930s and 1940s, could witness today's Christian Education program, he would be pleased to see that dedicated volunteers are teaching a new generation with the same degree of commitment as the teachers he led. Mary Ann Phillip served as CE Coordinator in the

---

[72] Answer: "Man's chief end is to glorify God and enjoy him forever."

mold of J.P. Frech in the early 1970s and was totally committed to the children. When she gave up her leadership role, she continued to teach several grade levels. Jan Jacewicz volunteered as Christian Education Coordinator in the late 1970s, and says, "I loved every minute of it. To be directly responsible for helping to teach and nurture children from cradle to college is a privilege." Linda Toner filled the same position from 1982 to 1985, and feels the same way. "Some may think these are thankless jobs, but I see them as nothing of the sort. There are no 'thankless' jobs when one is serving the Lord which is what all volunteers do in the context of Lewinsville." As soon as one volunteer is named, another comes to mind. Karen Hummel worked for about a year following Linda Toner.

Figure 31-Linda Toner

Education Redefined

Rev. Tad Wicker was called as Associate Pastor in 1987, and soon was deeply involved in the Christian Education program. With the assistance of his sister, Marsha Allen, a Youth Club was started in 1988. The plan called for Wednesday nights to be set aside for recreation, Bible Study, dinner and choir activities. For three years, more than sixty students, ranging from grades four to nine, participated in Youth Club.

Figure 32- By the 1980s, the first Puppet Ministry troupe was formed at Lewinsville.

The Christian Education program was growing—fast. Demands for youth and adult education, youth fellowship activities, Vacation Bible School, crib and preschool care were taxing volunteers to the limit. Session approved a request in 1988 to establish a new position—Director of Christian Education—and this time, the DCE would be paid a salary. Mary Hill was hired in December 1988 to work in a half-time capacity as Lewinsville's first paid professional Christian educator.

Mary resigned in 1990 to take a full-time position as DCE at Old Presbyterian Meeting House. She later assumed a part-time position as program manager for the Reformed Institute of Metropolitan Washington (another initiative begun by Lewinsville under the leadership of Lewinsville member Dr. Bruce Douglass). Mary was succeeded by Susan Seehaver in 1993. Her arrival led to a thorough evaluation of the children's Church School program. Perhaps the most important change that occurred during Susan's tenure was adoption of the Workshop Rotation Model as the curriculum for youth in grades one through six. Still in use today, the Workshop Rotation method has been adopted by Presbyterian churches across the nation.

Figure 33-Susan Seehaver

But always, the success of the CE program relied upon an army of volunteers from the membership, working closely with the CE Director, to inspire each generation with a new telling of the "old, old story."

For adults, Susan worked to strengthen the six-week module approach to include study of scripture, theology, world religions, Christian arts, ethics and public policy. Her teachers came primarily from the large pool of experts in the congregation, and occasionally, from outside specialists. It is not an overstatement to say that Susan Seehaver created a thriving Christian Education program that others sought to emulate as closely as possible. Sadly for Lewinsville, she resigned in November 2001, and Sallie R. White-Bishton served as Interim Director of Christian Education. Another volunteer, Linda Hagedorn, followed Sallie as Interim Director while a search committee completed its work. In November 2003, Allison G. Lineberger accepted Lewinsville's offer and began her great work. She was a perfect fit for the Lewinsville CE program. In 2013, Allison celebrated her tenth year as Lewinsville's Director of Christian Education.

Before Allison Lineberger, there was another Allison on our professional staff. Allison K. Nahr—"Allison-1" as she was known— became Director of Youth Ministries in May 2001 and accepted a large portfolio of responsibilities. "Allison-1" took over the education of Junior and Senior Highs, instruction of the Confirmand Class, and Youth Fellowship. And for the first time, Confirmands were paired with adult mentors, a practice that continues. Lewinsville bid her a sad farewell in March 2007 when she and her family moved back to their home state of Minnesota.

Reformed Institute of Metropolitan Washington (2003-present)

If Lewinsville did not know it before, the little white frame church in the woods of Northern Virginia realized it had come a long way when it created the Reformed Institute in 2003. Dr. Bruce Douglass, Lewinsville member, was the major impetus behind the founding of the Reformed Institute. He recruited several additional Presbyterian Churches from the National Capital Presbytery to the cause: Darnestown, Fairfax, Georgetown, Old Presbyterian Meeting House, Potomac, and Westminster. After three years, Fairfax withdrew its support, but was replaced by Immanuel, Heritage and Saint Mark. National Presbyterian was a sponsor from 2008 through 2010.

Figure 34-Bagpiper on Reformation Sunday

The Reformed Institute was created to promote understanding and deepen appreciation for the Reformed Tradition within Presbyterian churches in the Washington metropolitan area. The Institute provides a variety of programs that combine reliable, up-to-date information about the history of the Reformed Tradition with an ongoing concern for the challenges currently facing Presbyterian churches in the performance of their ministries. Rev. Pinder was a leader in establishing the Institute and strengthened it prior to his retirement. Rev. Deborah A. McKinley, called to Lewinsville in late 2008, has now joined the leadership of the Institute. Dr. Douglass continues to lead the Institute, and is a frequent adult education teacher at Lewinsville and other churches throughout the Presbytery.

**

Chapter Nine
Carry One Another's Burden

For decades the Ladies Aid Society was the real life blood of the church. Whenever something was needed or there was a financial deficit, the church turned to the Ladies Aid. A sumptuous dinner that attracted townsfolk as well as members would generally be enough to provide for any need. "It is quite possible," Dr. Gillespie wrote, "that the church would not be in existence today if it were not for the stewardship of time and talents of the Ladies Aid."[73]

Presbyterian Women

The Ladies Aid Society eventually changed its name to Presbyterian Women, a change that was made permanent with the reuniting of the northern (UPCUSA) and southern (PCUS) Presbyterian churches in 1983.

The first woman elected to Lewinsville's Session was Virginia F. Clarke in 1947. She was followed by six more female elders elected over the next twenty-two years. Between 1970 and 1975, the dam finally burst: twenty-three women became elders at Lewinsville. At the national level, in 1972, Lois H. Stair, a businesswoman from Wisconsin, became the first woman moderator of the Presbyterian General Assembly.

Traditionally, women were seen as deacons, teachers in Sunday School, and most frequently, as volunteers or support personnel in the church office. Today, women serve in positions of leadership throughout the church, Presbytery, Synod, and General Assembly.

---

[73] Ibid., *A Brief History*, p.26

In the last quarter of the twentieth century, three women were taken under the care of Lewinsville's Session in their preparation for ministry: Jane Quinn, Jane Harmes and Susan Kendall. All have been ordained. In the first decade of the twenty-first century, two more, Katie Cummings and Stephany Crosby, were ordained. Clearly, women have come a long way since Rev. C.B. McKee was forced to deal with the problem of a woman attempting to lead prayer in church in the mid-nineteenth century.

Deacons Reconstituted

The deacons were first formed at Lewinsville, June 21, 1942, dissolved in 1975, and finally reconstituted in 1993 with an even larger mission: Stephen Ministry.

Figure 35-First Pastoral Care Callers (left to right): Betty Palmer, Rev. Pinder, Georgia Sebestyen, Peggy Miller, Martha Britt, Rev. Smith, Marion Smith (Houser), Sally Carter

The need for reconstituting the Diaconate became apparent in 1983 when Session approved the creation of Pastoral Care Callers. The Callers, led by Sally Carter, had discovered that many of the people who came to their attention needed far more than financial assistance which had been typical of requests made in the past. Many were facing life challenges and changing circumstances that called for a wider range of support.

Deacons have always ministered to those in need as committed volunteers. With the training provided through the Stephen Minister program, deacons now minister as trained professionals. Typically, the training involves a week long course of study, including learning how to pray with those in need and how to develop appropriate listening skills. The goal is to "reach more people with Christian care than pastors can reach by themselves."[74] Once certified as a Stephen Minister and ordained, a deacon is assigned to someone in need. The deacons/Stephen Ministers are no less than twelve at any one time, nor more than eighteen.

ChristCare Groups Established

As the Stephen Ministry evolved over the years, ChristCare groups emerged. ChristCare is a part of the Stephen Ministry program and is designed to deepen spiritual development among persons meeting in small groups. Philip Cummings provided the impetus for their development when he headed a task force to study the need he perceived for members to develop stronger interpersonal connections and to deepen their relationship with Jesus Christ. Phil Cummings and Peg Baldauf were the first to attend training classes in St. Louis, May 1999.

Today there are seven ChristCare groups with more than seventy members participating. Groups typically consist of three to twelve people, and include at least one trained leader. Each ChristCare group decides as a unit the focus of its biblical study and the nature of its service or outreach.

ChristCare Groups have become an important part of Lewinsville's ministry due, in large measure, to their ability to build community. In a world where people often feel isolated from each other, there is a strong need to have a place where you are known, where you have family. In ChristCare Groups, people develop trust, love, and acceptance. Participants are able to share joys as well as serious struggles. New members find a place to connect, and longtime members find a place for continued growth.

---

[74] *The Church at Lewinsville at Millennium's Close*, p. 8

Social Group Connectivity

Social groups are mentioned here because they are as much a part of the fabric that holds us together and draws in new Christians as

Figure 36-Adult Club boat party, 1994

any of the formally organized ministries. There was the Young Adult Group which became the Boomers by 1987. They were a little younger than Second Saturday Set which got its start in 1972.

No one can remember the exact date when the Adult Club was started, but "the early 1960s" is "about right" according to Steve Stephenson. In other words, counting the period when it was known as the Couples Club, they have probably been around for more than sixty years.

And there were others. Lewinsville Singles was popular in the mid-1980s but was disbanded when most of its members got married. The Senior Adult Fellowship existed for those who had reached or passed retirement age. By 1991, a new group, Kids 'n Us, was established for parents with young children from birth to elementary school. It is perhaps a misnomer to describe these organizations as "social clubs" when they were—and are—so much more. All of them have been an important part of Lewinsville's culture of caring. Perhaps none is more emblematic of this culture than the Second Saturday Set.

Second Saturday Set (SSS)

War babies— born before, during and immediately after World War II—had a dramatic impact upon Lewinsville when they began arriving on Lewinsville's doorstep in the early 1950s. Most of them reached maturity in the period between 1958 and 1972. They and their children shared so many things in common that it is little wonder they bonded immediately and formed a strong social group, the Second Saturday Set, a group that has ministered as much to each other as to the church they chose. They came from extraordinarily disparate backgrounds— from flinty independent New Hampshire to the Bible Belt of the deep South, from New York to Alabama, from Minnesota to Mississippi—and quickly, the protestant Reformed Tradition that guided them in their youth became the faith around which their interests coalesced at Lewinsville. At one time, SSS included fifty couples and more than a dozen singles in its membership. In May 2011, the group celebrated its fortieth year of bonding.

Figure 37-Founding members of the Second Saturday Set in 2011

Perhaps even more remarkable, most of the founding members remain active at Lewinsville forty years later: Alan and Liz Stevens, Roy and Nancy Mitchell, Lois Dokken, Cathy and Bob Gaugler, Bob and Mary Ann Philipp, Doug McGuire.

**

Chapter Ten
Decently and In Order

P resbyterian churches are governed by elders, who convene regularly as an ordained group. Some have trustees. For a while, Lewinsville had both elders and trustees. Amzi Coe was the first elder, and Commodore Thomas ap Catesby Jones was the first trustee. As churches grow, they usually have need of deacons, but since Lewinsville did not experience significant growth until Rev. Gillespie arrived, a diaconate was not formed at the church until 1942.

First Up, and Then Down
   Throughout its history, Lewinsville has sought to tweak matters of governance in order to assure its ministry would be performed at the highest level of efficiency and efficacy. On January 7, 1898, the congregation decided the church should be governed by a constitution. Mrs. Lydia Dutrow and Mrs. Albert Mack were asked to work with Session to draft a constitution. When it was presented on February 22, 1898, it was unanimously adopted. "Although not carefully followed, it was in force until April 5, 1944, when the revised constitution was adopted by the congregation."[75] There is no evidence of either constitution in church files today.
   Just as those early constitutions were well intended at the time they were proposed, at least one modern change in governance also proved to be of questionable value.

---

[75] Ibid., *A Brief History*, p. 12

Session of Twenty-Eight Elders

During the tenure of Rev. Bill Tatum, the congregation decided to dissolve the Diaconate and merge its functions into the Session. The trustees were merged with Session as well. Session was responsible for the administration of all spiritual and civil matters.

> *"...to allow more efficient administration...and to encourage greater participation..."*

Eighteen members of Session soon became twenty-eight as a unicameral board was created in 1975 "to eliminate the lack of communication and the occasional tensions that have existed between the boards...to improve the quality of board membership, for the best talents of officers would be directed at all church matters...to allow more efficient administration...and to encourage greater participation by members of the congregation who would serve on a strong committee organization. Lastly, all board members would be elders, eliminating 'false distinctions between spiritual and temporal (corporate) affairs of the church.'"[76]

A unicameral board led to unintended consequences, however; most significantly, lengthy meetings with even more lengthy agendas that frequently did not end until well after midnight. This unwieldy mechanism was short-lived. By May 1981, the Session was reduced once again to eighteen members.

Today's elders are guided by a loose-leaf policy manual that contains all precedents, if any, for actions being considered. Elders no longer chair committees, and serve only as liaisons between ministry groups and the Session.[77] In 2003, Session was reduced still further from eighteen members to twelve, a number that has proven ideal for consideration of all issues. The change was initiated in 2004 by electing

---

[76] Lewinsville Newsletter, May 1972
[77] Six Ministry Groups: Worship, Christian Education, Parish Life and Care, Membership, Mission and Service, and Management.

four persons to serve as elders in the Class of 2007 and an equal number in succeeding years.

Foundation Established in 1985

The Lewinsville Presbyterian Church Foundation was established in May 1985 to manage the accumulation of capital assets that have been realized through the generosity of members and friends. The founding gift from the church was $23,418.18. Frances Grimes added $286,386.24 soon thereafter and the Foundation was off and running. The Foundation was established by Session as a Trust, governed by a board elected from the membership at large. For twenty years following its creation, the Foundation was led by Elder Michael Wachtel.

With a recognized expertise in managing funds in the permanent endowment, the Foundation was given the responsibility of managing monies set aside for committees and church-wide activities. It also processes all memorial gifts. By the end of 2012, the total of all funds managed, including funds for the music program, the Cemetery Fund, administrative accounts and memorials, was more than $1.8 million.

Foundation funds have been set aside to assist the church in funding capital improvements that are outside the annual operating budget. Foundation monies have made possible the purchase of "Peters Green," loans (later forgiven) that helped jumpstart the building of the Chesterbrook Residences, and many improvements to Lewinsville's physical plant, including a new computer system, carpeting and furniture for the youth center, extensive landscaping and exterior doors for St. Andrew's Hall, to list a few.

1846 Covenant Society Created (2009)

In October 2009, under the leadership of Rosalind Phillips, the Foundation announced its launching of the 1846 Covenant Society, a legacy organization created to build a spiritual legacy for the church that will strengthen and extend Lewinsville's mission and ministry for the benefit of future generations. Soon after the 1846 Covenant Society was announced, more than eighty individuals became charter members by indicating they have included the church and/or the Foundation in their estate planning. Lewinsville continues to add names to the 1846 Covenant Society annually.

**

Chapter Eleven
That Vision Thing

Periodically, Lewinsville has stopped to assess, take stock, and reflect, as it seeks to determine the vision God would have us follow to further his kingdom on Earth. The record is replete with such instances, formal and informal. Project '70 may have been the first recorded attempt to establish a long-term vision for the church. Under the leadership of Rev. Pinder, the entire congregation participated in a process to establish these goals: establish Alternative House for troubled teenagers; a pastoral counseling center in our former manse; an invitation to Alcoholics Anonymous to meet in Heritage Hall; a coffee house for young people in the basement of the old manse; and experimental worship services.

In 1972, Session set up two-member Listening Teams "to attend regular meetings of Lewinsville's fifteen boards, committees and other organizations in order to solicit ideas for the development of goals and priorities for the church in 1973."[78] It was more of an attempt to set budget priorities for the next year than to determine a true vision for the church.

A decade later, Session asked Robert Rayle to conduct his Sage Analysis, a process which queried each member and assimilated results and trends. Again, its primary purpose was not so much to look forward as it was to define current program areas Lewinsville should strengthen. From the Sage Analysis came the initiative for Session and pastors to

---

[78] Report of Mission Interpretation & Stewardship Committee, Don Robb, Chair, 1972

develop a "covenant-making process," an exercise to more clearly define the time and energy and focus of the pastors' ministry."[79]

In 1995, Elder Paul Phillips was asked to chair the Vision 2000 initiative, an attempt to develop a vision that would guide the church into the new century. In the mission statement developed over three months of intensive work involving the entire congregation, Lewinsville decided it should "connect with and nurture each other in order to foster a feeling of welcome; strengthen the bonds of community so that we can engage in evangelism and social outreach to all age groups in the church and beyond; share in joyful worship with varied music formats that meet the needs of our congregation, and provide different experiences for worship."[80]

Journey for Discernment

For two years prior to the retirement of Rev. Pinder in 2005, the congregation engaged in a Journey for Discernment. The goal was to develop a blue print that could be used as a spiritual guide for Lewinsville through its transition to new leadership, and perhaps, beyond. It was an intensive effort to involve all members of the church via small group gatherings in planning for Lewinsville's future. When the process was completed, Session adopted the following "callings" to lead Lewinsville in pursuit of deeper connections to God, the community, the world and each other:

- "Strengthen and expand small group ministries in order that deeper connections may be made between one another, Christ and the world;

---

[79] Annual Report, 1985
[80] 1997 Stewardship Report, *Reflecting on Visions 2000 Goals*

- Expand our understanding of mission as well as its purpose and scope (beyond traditional mission activities to include witnessing to the larger community as well as one-on-one sharing of personal faith), and generating greater awareness of mission opportunities;
- Interject more "heart" into worship and all aspects of Lewinsville's life (e.g., "prayers and concerns" time, and services of "healing and wholeness"); in the spirit of our Reformed Tradition, continue to instill our worship services with the holy, sacred, awesomeness of God;
- Focus all areas of ministry—worship, education, mission, small groups—on Christian formation (intentionally including the experiential along with the intellectual as a vital part of forming our faith understanding and Christian life);
- Embrace new ways to remain relevant to all demographic groups within the congregation (e.g., harnessing new technology such as "podcasting" and "blogging" to reach our youth via current interactive media, and offering supplemental services for a range of ages and interests);
- Be intentionally invitational in every aspect of church life."[81]

Over the years, Lewinsville has searched for a vision to guide it, searching, perhaps, for a way to enhance the vision the Apostle Paul wrote about in his letter to the church of Corinth. Paul wrote about seeing the church as a body made of many parts, each of which performs a specific function if the body is to remain healthy. Each part of the body is essential, with each part showing care and respect for all others. "For if one suffers, all suffer together; if one member is honored, all rejoice together. Now you are the body of Christ and each one of you is a part

---

[81] *Journey for Discernment*, Report to the Congregation, September 11, 2005

of it."[82] The same is as true today as it was in Paul's time. When people share this vision and give of their time, energy and possessions to the life and work of the church, the church comes alive and is able to reach out to minister to the needs of people everywhere. That's been the guiding essence of Lewinsville's vision, however defined, throughout its history.

Mission/Vision Statements Adopted in 2013

In 2010, a Visioning Task Force, consisting of eight members, was created by Rev. Debbie McKinley to take yet another look at Lewinsville's Vision/Mission. Its goal was to set a new course for the congregation that more accurately reflects the Vision and the Mission of Lewinsville as it enters the second decade of the twenty-first century. David Stahlman, chair of the Visioning Task Force, presented the results to Session.

---

[82] I Corinthians 12: 26-27

Mission
We are *Claimed* by God in Jesus Christ,
Called to live as a community of faith,
Sent to participate in the unfolding of God's kingdom on earth.

Approved by Session, June 12, 2012

Vision
As we approach our 175th year of ministry, the people of Lewinsville Presbyterian Church celebrate the gifts and opportunities given to us. We strive to build on our heritage of Christian discipleship to serve God and all creation.

We strengthen our congregation as we:

- Worship God in ways that engage the spirit, mind, heart and body.
- Educate and form disciples in Christian faith.
- Care for one another with the compassion of Jesus Christ.
- We participate in Christ's mission in the world— to redeem and transform all creation—as we:
    - Extend our legacy of care to vulnerable older adults and their families.
    - Reach out to the youth of northern Virginia, ushering them into a healthy, vibrant, productive adulthood.
    - Provide a forum for civil public policy discourse and, as faithful Christians, address social justice issues.
    - Become a recognized Christian presence in the emerging Tysons-urban center.

Claimed,
    Called,
        Sent
            by Jesus Christ, who alone is head of the Church.

Approved by Session April 9, 2013

Session has since created a Strategic Planning Group[83] to develop a plan to meet the goals set forth, or as someone said, "put wheels under it." The congregation looks forward, with excited anticipation, to the result of the group's imagination, courage and faith.

**

---

[83] Strategic Planning Group 2013: Doug Cochrane, Jim Edmondson (Chair), Irene Foster, Roy Mitchell, Adrian Steel, Linda Toner, and Tonya Deyo. David Morrison was an original member of the committee but resigned when he entered seminary.

Chapter Twelve
A New Millennium Begins

The first decade of the new millennium at Lewinsville Presbyterian Church is best characterized as one of milestone changes. It was clear from the start that this was not going to be another Donna Reed decade. In 1999, Lewinsville became one of only ten churches in the National Capital Presbytery to launch a website, and that was just the beginning. Second, Lewinsville experienced a nearly 100 percent turnover in personnel during the decade. And third, Lewinsville, working with two other faith communities, built and opened an assisted living facility, an accomplishment signifying the underlying strength within the church to enthusiastically meet new challenges as they are presented.

Digital Age Arrives

Lewinsville's early entry into the digital age in 1999 was made possible through the generosity of three donors who provided funds needed to design and launch www.lewinsville.org. The Lewinsville website is the place where many new members begin their search for information about Lewinsville Presbyterian Church. The site is visited on average 250 times per month. The site includes videos of Sunday sermons and scripture readings (edited for online viewing), online sign-up forms for church activities and the latest information on each activity.

90 || Pilgrims and Pioneers Always

A partner to the website is Lewinsville's Facebook page where members receive alerts, news of activities and events within the life of the congregation.

A second partner to the website is Lewinsville's Flickr page where hundreds of photos of people and events from Lewinsville are stored. Someone called it "a photo album for the Lewinsville family," and, indeed, it is.

Finally, in 2010, new digital signage was installed in St. Andrews Hall and another immediately outside the church office. Both digital displays contain information about forthcoming events and photos of recent church activity. All four of these digital services are handled by two member volunteers.

"…the computer is already full of data…"

The first computer was installed in the church office in late 1984—an IBM 8088.[84] In the annual report of 1984, the church administrator reported that the computer "is already full of data entered by volunteers." Today, every staff position is networked and files are shared. Online access is wireless, and more communication tools are being designed to reach our congregation electronically. Communication with the extended family of Lewinsville congregants will soon involve all available social media.

Perhaps the most important asset social media have brought to the church is the enormous digital record accumulated, reflecting the broad range of Lewinsville's ministry. It is a record that will be used in the future, undoubtedly, to demonstrate that the "little white church at Barrett's Crossroads" always remains faithful to its 1846 heritage.

Major Personnel Changes

While the digital world was being introduced to Lewinsville in the first decade of the new century, enormous change was taking place in Lewinsville's professional leadership. Some retired, some moved on, and a new generation of leaders settled in at Lewinsville Church.

"In a world of change, pastor and people need to share in the ministry more than ever…"

---

[84] The IBM 8088 computer was bought with funds solicited for that purpose and a $2,000 loan from the cemetery fund. Elder David Dawson led the effort to purchase the first computer.

First, the retirees:

Rev. Gary George Pinder (1968 – 2005) Senior Pastor

Figure 38-Rev. Pinder carries cross gifted by the Arnolds into church

Rev. Pinder retired in October 2005, capping a career of thirty-seven years in the pulpit at Lewinsville. When he arrived at Lewinsville in 1968, Rev. Pinder was asked what advice he would give to his new congregation. His response was telling. "I am well aware that the church is not the ministers but belongs jointly to the ministers and the congregation. Together we are the 'Laos,' (Greek-Latin), 'The people of God.' We are called to share our life in Christ together. In a world of change, pastor and people need to share in the ministry more than ever."[85] And thus it was for thirty-seven years of Rev. Pinder's ministry.

J. Franklin Clark (1967 – 2004) Minister of Music

At his retirement in 2004, J. Clark, Minister of Music, was the longest serving member of Lewinsville's professional staff. The sanctuary was filled to overflowing on J.'s last Sunday to celebrate and thank J. for his thirty-seven years at Lewinsville. The festivities continued at the McLean

---

[85] Lewinsville Letter, April 29, 1971, Gary G. Pinder, p. 5

Community Center in the afternoon. "My goal, always, was to make music an enjoyable art form dedicated to the glory of God while helping to prepare our children, youth, and adults for future participation as worship leaders at Lewinsville," J. wrote in his final report to the congregation.[86] In retirement, J. moved to Atlanta to be closer to his family but not before accepting a part-time ministry of music at Druid Hills Presbyterian Church. At this writing, he continues on the part-time organ staff at the Episcopal Cathedral of St. Philip in Atlanta.

Rev. Dr. Mark Andrews (1995 – 2002) Parish Associate

Dr. Andrews, parish associate, came to us in 1995 following the resignation of Rev. Tad Wicker. Wherever Mark served in his sixty-two years of ministry, he made a lasting impact. Lewinsville was no exception. In addition, his "Prayers of the People" were always eloquent and humble petitions that lifted up the hearer even as they asked for Divine intervention on behalf of those in need. Many encouraged Mark to collect those prayers and publish them for the benefit of future generations.

There seemed to be no end to his talents. Who could have imagined that Mark would take the simple request of asking members and guests to register their attendance in the "little red book" in the pews and turn it into one of the most anticipated announcements of the worship service? He always began with a story that had a life lesson somewhere within it, and eventually Mark used the story to introduce the exercise of signing one's name in the pew pad.

---

[86] Annual Report, January 2004, p. 4

Mark was first an Army Chaplain during World War II, then a full-time pastor at three different churches—La Crosse, Wisconsin; Erie, Pennsylvania; Redlands, California—before moving to Kansas to become Synod Executive. Along the way, he found time to play an instrumental role in drafting the Confession of 1967. At age sixty-five, he thought it was time to retire so he moved to Swarthmore, Pennsylvania, but even there he found a way to counsel and serve thirteen churches. Finally, Mark moved to Maryland to be closer to his daughter, Dr. Susan Andrews, (future moderator of the General Assembly). She was pastor of Bradley Hills Presbyterian Church at the time. Lewinsville welcomed him warmly, and he seamlessly integrated his energy and faith into every aspect of life at Lewinsville.

In 2000, Dr. Andrews marked his sixtieth year of ordained ministry, and a year later, he and Elizabeth celebrated their sixtieth wedding anniversary. Upon his final retirement in 2002, Lewinsville gave him a new title, Parish Associate Emeritus, a title that meant, "You will always be welcome among your family at Lewinsville." Dr. Andrews and his wife, Elizabeth, are now buried in the church cemetery among the many saints who preceded them in strengthening the ministry of Lewinsville Presbyterian Church.

Verna White Chenault (1990 – 2012) Church Secretary

Verna White celebrated twenty-two years of service as Church Secretary when she retired at the end of January 2012. Verna's winsome smile and impeccable English accent welcomed everyone who entered the office. Her calm demeanor was her way of staying focused on solving the problem *du jour*.

Sidney Jones (1979-2011) Building Superintendent

Every organization has at least one person on board like Sidney Jones. He's the one you cannot do without. When Sidney retired at end of summer 2011, he had played that role at Lewinsville for thirty-two years. "Sid is a man who has always taken life as a gift from God and who has devoted his life to his family and to serving Christ's church," said Pastor Emeritus Gary Pinder. "Whether pastoring his own congregation or caring for the Lewinsville congregation as our Building Superintendent, Sid has been committed to using his knowledge and skills to contribute to and care for God's people."

One who moved on:

Dr. Edward Alan Moore (2005-2010) Minister of Music

J. Clark was followed by Dr. Edward Moore, a gifted and talented organist and choir director, who quickly demonstrated his many musical gifts and leadership skills. Music has always played a central role in the worship and ministry of Lewinsville Church. Ed not only continued the fine musical legacy J. Clark established, he built upon it. He was an energetic and creative leader of all choirs, ringers, and guest musicians. Today, he is Organist and Music Director at East Liberty Presbyterian Church, Pittsburgh, Pennsylvania.

96 || Pilgrims and Pioneers Always

A new generation of leaders arrived:

Allison Gordon Lineberger (2003—present) Director of Christian Education

Allison Lineberger joined the staff at Lewinsville in November 2003 from Second Presbyterian Church, Knoxville, Tennessee, where she worked five years as Director of Children's Ministries. At Lewinsville, she has followed the well-established tradition of excellence set by Mary Hill and Susan Seehaver in preceding years.

Rev. Emily Berman D'Andrea (2002—present) Associate Pastor for Christian Formation

In January 2002, the congregation voted to call Rev. Emily Berman D'Andrea as Associate Pastor. At the time of her call, she was serving Burke Presbyterian Church, Burke, Virginia, where she was involved in its spiritual growth and development. Prior to receiving the call to ministry, Emily worked on the US Senate Environment and Public Works Committee. She completed her Master of Divinity degree from Princeton Theological Seminary in 1997 and accepted her first call, Burke Presbyterian. At Lewinsville, she picked up the pastoral duties of Mark Andrews and never missed a beat. In the fall of 2002, Emily initiated a Taizé worship service at Lewinsville, held on the first Sunday evening of the month. The Taizé service of song and silence is based on the daily worship model of the ecumenical community of brothers in Burgundy, France.

Emily chairs the Presbytery's Personnel Committee and serves as a member of the Committee on Ministry Clearance Team One (with

Elder Bruce Douglass), examining ministers seeking positions in churches within the Presbytery.

Rev Deborah A. McKinley (2008—present) Pastor/Head of Staff

Figure 39-Debbie was installed as Pastor/Head of Staff at Lewinsville on February 22, 2009

An extensive two-year search led Lewinsville's Pastor Nominating Committee to Old Pine Presbyterian, a small urban church in the heart of Philadelphia, where the PNC found Rev. Debbie McKinley. She accepted the call in September 2008 and preached her first sermon as Pastor/Head of staff in November. She is the first woman to lead Lewinsville.

Rev. McKinley was ordained in 1982 at Pine Street Presbyterian, Harrisburg, Pennsylvania, and served that congregation nine years as Assistant Pastor, then Associate Pastor. Through the years, she served on the national staff of PC(USA) as Associate for Worship, and was an editorial consultant on the Book of Common Worship. In that capacity, she traveled the nation, introducing this resource to Presbyterian churches.

Debbie serves on the Princeton Theological Seminary Board of Trustees (Class of 2014), chairing the Committee on Trustees (a governance and nominating committee) and recently participated in the work of the Presidential Search Committee. She also chairs a Presbytery Organizational Review Task Force.

Michael Divine (2012—present) Director of Music Ministries

Michael Divine was chosen to follow Ed Moore and his arrival marked a departure from the tradition of seeking an organist to head the music program. He is a vocalist extraordinaire.

Michael graduated from a joint program at Luther Seminary and St. Olaf College in Minnesota with a Master's Degree in Sacred Music. During his degree studies, Michael worked in four churches, and was choir director at the United Methodist Church of Anoka, Minnesota, before coming to Lewinsville. In addition to his excellent credentials in training and experience, Michael has a creative way of weaving music into nearly all facets of Lewinsville's life. He is a thorough professional who is already nurturing and developing the talents of Lewinsville choirs.

Kate Satterstrom (2012—present) Director of Youth Ministries

Kate Satterstrom was recruited to join Lewinsville as Director of Youth Ministries following the resignation of Doug Miller, 2010-2012. Miller was preceded by Amanda Tomkins, 2008-2010, and Allison K. Nahr, 2001-2007.

Kate graduated from Princeton Theological Seminary, with a dual degree: M.Div. and M.A. with a concentration in Youth Ministry. All of Kate's field education experience has been in youth ministry. She continued as a volunteer youth advisor at Nassau Presbyterian Church, Princeton, NJ, after her field education experience was completed. Kate's responsibilities include planning and oversight of youth fellowship, youth Sunday School and confirmation, youth mission trips (including Winter and Summer Mission Projects). She is also charged with reaching out and creating programming for college age and other young adults, in collaboration with the Youth Council.

Gary Fitzgerald (2012—present) Church Administrator

Gary Fitzgerald began his ministry with Lewinsville in September 2012. He followed John Bean who served from 2008 to 2012. Before Bean, Lewinsville was blessed with the extraordinary talents of Bob Clark.

Bob was Church Administrator from 2001 to July 2008 when he transferred to Old Presbyterian Meeting House. Fortunately, he decided to become a member of the Lewinsville congregation. Gary Fitzgerald follows in the tradition of both John Bean and Bob Clark. In addition to his administrative skills, Gary is an accomplished cellist, organist, and pianist. In 2004, he decided to devote himself to full-time church work. Gary expanded his vocation to include Church Administration in 2004.

Figure 40-Bob Clark

Sandy Albrecht (2001—present) Church Office Manager

When Pam Crosby retired as Pastor's Secretary in the summer of 2001, Sandy Albrecht was hired to assume Pam's duties. Rev. McKinley expanded Sandy's duties and changed her title to Church Office Manager. As anyone who has reason to contact the church office knows, Sandy is the "go to" person to get anything done—anything at all.

Steve Kirkland (2008—present) Sexton

As Sidney Jones approached retirement, Gordon Dunning was hired to assist him as Evening Sexton, but when Gordon died suddenly in September 2008, the church, fortunately, found Steve Kirkland. Steve has performed with the same dedication and work ethic that Sidney Jones exhibited for thirty-two years. Steve has now been given the duties of Church Sexton.

Chesterbrook Residences Opened in 2007

When Lewinsville made a commitment to reach out to the community for a deeper connection in the 1960s, hardly anyone imagined such an ambitious list of capital projects would be in Lewinsville's future. In the 1970s, it was Lewinsville Retirement Residence; in the 1980s, it was renovation and expansion of the church facility itself; in the 1990s, it was the construction of Lewinsville East; and in the 2000s, it was the Chesterbrook Residences assisted living project.

Figure 41-Chesterbrook Residences, 2007

The Chesterbrook project started early in the decade and nearly consumed the decade before it was opened. Jerry Hopkins, parish associate, became a principal leader in the project, but had significant support from Rev. Pinder, Jim and Jane Edmondson, and the entire congregation.

The National Capital Presbytery asked Lewinsville in 2000 to explore the feasibility of developing an assisted living facility on a five-acre tract of land occupied at the time by Chesterbrook Presbyterian Church. With many of its elderly members declining in numbers, the little church notified the Presbytery it was preparing to disband. Lewinsville excitedly took up the challenge. After all, it had successfully wormed its way through the government bureaucracy at the local, state and federal level a few years earlier and emerged with the successful founding of Lewinsville Retirement Residence adjacent to church property.

Presbytery's request led Lewinsville on a bumpy and bruising journey of nearly seven years. The mission was to build, own and operate an affordable assisted living residence for the elderly of Northern Virginia. Architects were asked to provide for a mix of residents with incomes from very low to those high enough to afford market rates. Two other faith communities became integral partners along the way: Temple Rodef Shalom and Immanuel Presbyterian Church.

Ground was broken, May 10, 2006, for Chesterbrook Residences. Among those participating were: Lewinsville's Jerry Hopkins, President of the Chesterbrook Residences board of directors; Jane Edmondson, Secretary, CRI; and Jim Edmondson, CRI Development Committee Chair.

With the talent of a large cadre of experts in real estate development, law, civic affairs and financing, the doors were opened in the fall of 2007 to a $13.3 million facility with ninety-seven units, a new home for 105 residents. The dedication was held in February 2008 with many of the principals who contributed to the project's success present, including Lewinsville Pastor Emeritus, Rev. Gary Pinder, who served as principal liaison among all interests throughout the process.

Figure 42-Chesterbrook Residences Dedication Ceremony, February 2008

**

Chapter Thirteen
Making New Disciples

Billboards bring few new Christians to the faith. To make a new disciple of Christ, "Show, don't tell" has proven to be one of the best ways to express one's faith and connect with the community.

As Rev. Gillespie said, "In the 1940s, the Ladies Aid Society was known for its culinary skills and frequently held dinners to which the entire community was invited." Lewinsville Christians have always sought creative ways to connect with the community and welcome others into the body of Christ.

Figure 43-1979 billboard across Chain Bridge Road

Through the years reaching out to strengthen Lewinsville's connection with the community has become a well-established tradition. From 1986 to 1998, The Lewinsville Players performed regularly in Fellowship Hall and at the Alden Theatre in the McLean Community Center. The first dramatic production was The Curious Savage, presented in Fellowship Hall in November 1986.[87] That was followed by an original play written by Pam Lawson, based on Frank Gapp's history of Lewinsville. Lawson's play was even presented outdoors on McLean Day. At its peak, thirty-five dedicated thespians counted themselves among the Players. Many of the Players also participated annually in The Lewinsville Follies, a broad display of performing artistry drawn from the congregation.

Figure 44-Lewinsville Players John Thomas and Bob Bender

Sooner or later, everyone had an opportunity to get in on the act. Marion Stedman organized The Lewinsville Lights, a Clown Ministry, in the mid-1980s that performed CE Festival Sunday at Lewinsville, nearby Vienna Presbyterian Church, and even made appearances in the children's wing of Fairfax Hospital. In addition to Marion Stedman, clowns included Lois Dokken, Martha Britt, Lynda Briscoe, Jean Ferguson, Cathy Gaugler and Sally Trout McKeown.

Today, local residents are likely to encounter bikers from Lewinsville on one of the many bike paths available in the Northern Virginia area. The Lewinsville Bikers proudly wear T-shirts identifying them as members of the church.

Of course, there is McLean Day when the entire church parking lot becomes an oasis from the heat for thousands attending the festivities in nearby Lewinsville Park.

---

[87] Other productions: Night Must Fall, An Evening of Melodrama, The Rich Czech Murders, Let's Murder Marsha, and Triple Play (Widow's Mite; I'm Herbert; Good Night, Caroline). Triple Play was favorably reviewed by the Washington Post.

Figure 45-W&OD Bike Path, Vienna 2011

Figure 46-Mike Deese at bat

Every fall, the Lewinsville Sluggers participate in one of several civic leagues in the area. Their won/loss record has never been stellar, but they always demonstrate to the world that Lewinsville Christians know how to have fun.

Once a list like this gets started, it is difficult to stop listing the many ways Lewinsville reaches out to the community. A relatively new venture is the fresh produce our gardeners are growing every year for the Share organization.

Figure 47-SHARE Garden Plot - Lewinsville gardeners

106 || Pilgrims and Pioneers Always

And from time to time, even our founder, Commodore Thomas ap Catesby Jones drops by to remind us of our heritage and to encourage our efforts to make new disciples of Christ, deepen our spiritual engagement, and improve our understanding of what it means to live the Christian faith at the church he founded in 1846.

Figure 48-"Commodore Thomas ap Catesby Jones," 1790-1858 [John Thomas]

**

Chapter Fourteen
Saints and Sinners

In the end, the history of Lewinsville is not about numbers—the rise and fall of membership, the increase and decrease in budgets, the facilities built or expanded, the number of choirs, the record of leadership and personnel changes. It is, and always has been, about the saints and sinners sitting in the pews, and the role they have played in the unfolding of God's kingdom at Barrett's Crossroads.

There was Tom Stedman whose skilled hands and master craftsmanship are evident throughout the church today. The three-panel church photo directory in St. Andrews Hall is one example of his fine craftsmanship. Tom was a quiet man who let his hands express his great faith. He would have made a fine member of Chuck Scheffey's Barnacled Beavers.

None who knew Howard Salzman will ever forget how his deep intellect opened minds and expanded views of the world each time he was engaged in conversation. Thanks to his wife, Shirley, the Salzman Lecture series exists today and enables the conversations he started to continue.

Many remember the contribution of Sally Carter. Sally worked with Rev. Pinder in the 1980s and 1990s to establish Pastoral Care Callers, the forerunner organization to today's Stephen Ministers.

Farther back, Alda Mack was an anchor of the faith who taught several generations of Lewinsville children in the 1930s and 1940s. Lewinsville has known many teachers like her, educators who come every Sunday, sharing their faith in the classes they teach, without expecting thanks or special recognition, and whose personal lives offer the children the best role models they could find.

And when Elaine Stewart took over preparation of floral arrangements for Sunday worship, a professional standard was set for that weekly task. The tradition of excellence in floral design that Elaine established has continued for the past twenty-five years under a committee led by Pam Deese, and the creative women who serve with her.

Nearly every reader would have at least one person to nominate for inclusion on this list, and all nominated would be worthy of it. There would be Pam Lawson, Ethelmae Page and J. Clark who created original musical scores and dramatic productions for the worship service, and Sally McKeown who introduced liturgical dance to accompany Scripture reading, and, of course, the volunteers who participate today in the Extended Communion program and minister to those who are unable to attend worship services. There would be Bob Gaugler, budget cognoscente, who has stepped in to fulfill the duties of Church Administrator whenever a vacancy existed; Alan Stevens, longest serving member of the board of directors of LRR (thirty-three years!); and Bruce Douglass, who, along with Rev. Pinder, founded the Reformed Institute in 2003. Bruce continues to lead and teach for the Institute today.

The history of Lewinsville is best told through the lives of these and others, known and unknown, who unreservedly shared their lives, their talents, and their faith with all with whom they came in contact. For many whose names are mentioned here, the sharing continues.

"...This is Lewinsville Presbyterian Church."

Now, there has to be a place where the history stops, where a period is placed and the book is closed. Yes—but not today. The story of Lewinsville cannot be finished, so long as two or three Christians gather at the spot where the church was nearly destroyed during the Civil War, where the congregation spurned the idea of selling out to the

Methodists in 1870, where the stovepipe fell on a sparse congregation in 1923 and resolve was strengthened to keep the doors open, where the unexpected gift was received in 1990 and a financial crisis averted, where faith in an unseen God was, and is, practiced in the midst of great doubt. This is Lewinsville Presbyterian Church.

And this is the place where Lewinsville is creating new disciples of Jesus Christ today, where new Christians and members of longstanding are working to develop deeper connections to God, to Christ, to the world, and to each other. This story is far from over. If Lewinsville's past is any precursor to what lies ahead, surely the congregation should look forward with great anticipation to a continuation of the story, and the publishing of yet another installment of Lewinsville's great heritage in years to come.

"Praise God from whom all blessings flow..."

**

Afterword
Serving Christ in a Nanotube World

Most laypersons know very little about carbon nanotubes, but, if scientists are correct, that is about to change. Scientists predict nanotubes are going to make lives a lot easier in the near future. Research in nanotechnology is done using a nanometer, a standard unit of measure that is a billionth of a meter—barely the size of ten hydrogen atoms in a row. Nanotubes are supposed to make paint that doesn't peel, drugs that absorb faster, cars that resist dents. The list goes on. Extraordinary products are in our future and the many ways they may change our lives cannot be imagined by most laypersons.

Through all the changes thrust upon our lives at Lewinsville, we have always been certain in the knowledge that God's amazing Grace has not changed and will not change. That's the assurance we have from Holy Scripture. But our two jobs, kids' sports, credit card, text messaging, online all the time, reschedule, eat it now, go to bed, get up, do it all again lives often leave us spiritually hungry, with a deep feeling of disconnectedness from the things that are important to us.

How does Lewinsville fit into the world of 2013 and beyond? How do we help shape this new world and not have it shape us?

Do we evolve, or do we stick to the status quo—the traditional church school, sermon in the pulpit on Sunday, youth meeting on Sunday night, choir on Thursday night? Or do we look for new ways to connect. We are not the fledgling young church anymore, sitting on the countryside of Northern Virginia, waiting for the influx of families that will provide the source of our enormous growth.

The challenges we face are quite different today. Consider the young single mother who slips into the back pew on Sunday morning wishing we offered a more convenient time for her to attend so she could ask her questions about Christianity. And she has many. But she is working two jobs, raising a young daughter and trying to finish her education, or maybe, pay for the education she has already received. She slips out before the benediction with the feeling that most of the churches she visits are out of sync with her life.

How do we help this young woman and others new to us become more than spiritual tourists, traveling through life without deeply held Christian convictions? How do we create an environment that addresses the needs of vulnerable youth in our midst? And don't forget those Boomers; they are now seventy million strong and starting to overwhelm services for the elderly. How do we help the young and the old in our society discover the depth of life and the richness of faith the Reformed Tradition offers?

The microscopic nanotube holds enormous promise for us but so does the mustard seed of faith within each of us. Both are very small and very powerful. Only a mustard seed size step of faith is necessary to continue the legacy left in trust to us by the pilgrims and pioneers of 1846.

Sometimes, the small step we take in faith, as Marie Lewis suggested, is the step hardly noticed except by God, but it becomes the step that sets our church on fire.

- ❖ When Session bought the Hammond/Eglin property in 1967, no one knew that small faith step would result in a retirement home for 144 residents.

- ❖ When Rev. Pinder took a group of young people to work one summer on the Pine Ridge Indian Reservation, he could not have imagined that that small step of faith would soon become more than fifty youth and adults on an annual summer trek to a Habitat site.

❖ When the first ChristCare Group met at Lewinsville, few placed much faith in its staying power, or noticed its potential for influencing lives. No one imagined that today there would be seven ChristCare groups involving more than one-fourth of the congregation in regular gatherings.

Lewinsville has never been a church to bless the status quo and only tinker around the edges. In reading Frank Gapp's 1976 history of Lewinsville and the 2000 update by Minerva Andrews and Marian O'Brien, one finds no timid people in Lewinsville's history.

In the tradition of those great pilgrims and pioneers who set our course in 1846, let us pray that the Lewinsville faith community will be bold enough to ask, "What else, what new, what better—can we do to remain faithful to the Gospel in these nanotube times?"

**

Acknowledgements

At a time before computers and the Internet were available to assist research, Frank W. Gapp devoted his shoe leather and personal time to the pursuit of Lewinsville's history in libraries, historical societies, family wills, state and county records, biographies of Virginia's early leaders, and countless personal documents loaned for his research. His booklet, The Church at Lewinsville, published in 1976 for the 130th anniversary of the church's founding, remains a valuable  compendium of detail surrounding the formative years that cannot be found in any other record. Frank was a member from 1948 until his death in 2003.

 In 2001, Minerva W. Andrews and Marian J. O'Brien crafted an update to the Gapp book to include the twenty-year period of 1976 to 2001. The Church at Lewinsville at Millennium's Close, as written by Andrews and O'Brien is a comprehensive literary work, from which the author has borrowed extensively and for which he is grateful.

The author also is indebted to Rev. Franklin B. Gillespie whose painstaking research through hundreds of scattered documents enabled him to piece together early church history in 1946. A Brief History of Lewinsville Presbyterian Church was written by Rev. Gillespie for Lewinsville's Centennial celebration, but will be always an invaluable resource for anyone interested in learning more about the firm foundation upon which the little white church at Barrett's Crossroads was built.

My thanks also to Jeffrey Kidwell, son of longtime member, Maynard Kidwell, who generously offered photos his father took of the original church before, during, and after it was disassembled in 1955; and to Carolyn Gillespie LeVan, daughter of Rev. Gillespie, who offered miscellaneous photos of congregational life taken during the 1940s when her father was Pastor at Lewinsville. Her contribution enhanced the telling of this story, and contributed immeasurably to its accuracy, filling in large gaps, and correcting factual misunderstandings.

Sincere appreciation is extended to editors Cathy Gaugler, Nancy Mitchell and Rosalind Phillips whose keen eyes, sharp pencils and gentle editorial nudging kept the author consistent and as accurate as his years and memory will allow.

B. Roland McElroy
October 2013

**

Appendix I
First Trustee: Commodore Thomas ap Catesby Jones

Commodore Thomas ap Catesby Jones began his naval career as a young lieutenant prior to the War of 1812. Through his pre-war service in the Gulf of Mexico, he created a distinguished record of service that included suppressing piracy, smuggling, and slave trading.[88] He was, therefore, perfectly positioned to participate in the defense of New Orleans when the War of 1812 broke out.

Jones' Role in War of 1812

Figure 49-Commodore Thomas ap Catesby Jones

Although the Americans enjoyed several early victories, they were stunned when the British stormed Washington and burned the Capitol and White House.[89] Emboldened by such quick success, the British turned their attention to Fort McHenry, in Baltimore's harbor. A small garrison of stalwart Americans defended the fort on the night of September 13, 1814. The Americans mounted a strong defense and prevented the British from gaining the strategic advantage Fort McHenry could provide. American forces not only survived the night, but by dawn, they were cheering as British naval

---

[88] Gapp, *The Church at Lewinsville*, p. 6
[89] President James Madison and his wife, Dolley, sought refuge with their longtime friends, William and Henrietta Maffitt at *Salona*.

vessels retreated from Baltimore harbor. The British advance was stopped.

But the war was not over.

Lieutenant Jones of Lewinsville, Virginia, was about to get his first real taste of the war. On December 12, 1814, three months after the Fort McHenry battle, a large British fleet prepared an assault on New Orleans. They anchored in the Gulf of Mexico to the east of Lake Pontchartrain and Lake Borgne. Facing them was a small flotilla of American gunboats under the command of Jones. Lieutenant Jones' assignment: delay the British commander as long as he could. Two days later, Jones and his five gunboats faced 1,200 British seamen as their longboats entered the shallow waters of Lake Borgne. The British longboats were disadvantaged because they ran aground frequently, but the American gunboats were simply outmanned. In the brief fight that ensued, Jones and his men were overwhelmed by the sheer number of British seamen and forced to surrender, but not before inflicting significant casualties: seventeen killed, seventy-seven wounded.[90]

Jones was shot in his left shoulder. He carried the bullet the rest of his life, and never regained the full use of his arm. Jones thought he had failed in his mission, but General Andrew Jackson praised him for his bravery and honored him for his success in carrying out the mission. General Jackson, with the help of pirate Jean Lafitte and his men, soon defeated the British and brought the War of 1812 to a close.

Later, Commodore Jones was assigned to the United States Pacific Squadron, a command he held from 1841 to 1843 when he retired to his beloved *Sharon* in Virginia. Soon, he found himself fully engaged in local business matters and immersed in the founding of Lewinsville Presbyterian Church.

---

[90] Wikipedia, http://en.wikipedia.org/wiki/Battle_of_New_Orleans

Appendix I: Thomas ap Catesby Jones || 119

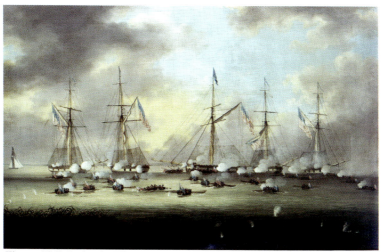

Figure 50-Painting by Thomas L. Hornbrook depicting British attack on American gunboats commanded by Lt. Thomas ap Catesby Jones, U.S.N., December 12, 1814.

**

Appendix II
History of the Lewinsville Organ

Figure 51-Prince Co. reed organ

Lewinsville's first organ was a small reed organ manufactured by Prince and Company of Buffalo, New York. Vintage ads from The American Farmer indicate it was sold widely from the 1860s to the late 1880s. According to one advertising claim, the Melodeon, as it was known, could play 609 notes!

In the first decade of the twentieth century a second reed organ, manufactured by the Estey Organ Company of Brattleboro, Vermont, was purchased and served the church well until 1938 when the Storm family gave the church a small Moller organ in memory of family members.[91] The tired Estey reed organ was moved to Dunham Hall where it was adopted by the Sunday School.[92]

Figure 52-Estey reed organ

---

[91] For many years, the Storm family operated a dairy farm near the church and was a force in Fairfax politics from the 1880s well into the twentieth century. Ten members of the Storm family are buried in the church cemetery.
[92] The original Prince reed organ is on display in the Chapel and the Estey reed organ can be found in the Parlor.

Figure 53-Moller organ

"The Moller had three ranks of pipes that were unified to make it seem larger," J. Clark recalled, "and it was placed in the left chamber above the console." The Moller had its limitations, according to Clark, who pushed for a replacement organ as soon as he arrived.

Figure 54-Moller organ pipes

Figure 55-In 1967, the choir was divided on both sides of the chancel so that one side had to look up into a large mirror to follow the organist as he conducted.

The Moller was replaced in 1968 when the church bought an organ built by the Casavant Frères firm of St-Hyacinthe, Quebec. It had two manuals and thirty-eight ranks. "The Casavant organ was placed on the wall with the choir and console on the floor," Clark said.

Figure 56-Casavant organ pipes

"The funny thing was that the original entry door on the right was lower than the first step up to the choir riser and we were constantly bumping our heads. Since the pipes were directly behind the top row of the choir, we had to install Plexiglas to keep little hands from reaching into the chamber."

Although the Casavant served Lewinsville well, by 1985, the Casavant was showing its age, requiring frequent and costly repairs. Nancy and Roy Mitchell decided the music ministry of Lewinsville would be enhanced significantly by a new organ, and they turned to the Gress-Miles Pipe Organ Company of Princeton, New Jersey for their gift. The organ they donated had three manuals and played music literature from all periods. J. Clark summarized his evaluation of the principal instruments he played while at Lewinsville: "The Storm organ could not play the literature well; it was not Baroque. The Casavant was more Baroque, and the Gress-Miles was more Romantic."

Figure 57-J. Clark at the Gress-Miles organ, 1986

When the Gress-Miles organ was installed, only the pipes from the Casavant organ were retained. "We revoiced all of the pipes of the Casavant," Clark said, "and increased the organ to 38 ranks of pipes. The pipe work was placed in the original two chambers and the choir loft was redesigned to accommodate a growing choir program." The JC trumpet was added in memory of Jimmie Clark, J.'s mother and Charlie Herseth, Judy Herseth's husband. Later a Zimbelstern (small bell), was added in memory of J.'s father. The Bombarde 8' and the Trumpet 4' were added in 1997. Altogether, there were 2,300 pipes in use by the Gress-Miles organ.

Figure 58-Carole Huston at the Gress-Miles organ, 2013

On the 25th anniversary of the Mitchell gift, a task force was formed to address needed repairs and improvements. Members of the task force included Roy and Nancy Mitchell, Judy Herseth, Dale Hodges, and Bob Johnson (representing the Worship Ministry Group). Dr. Ed Moore, former Director of Music Ministries, also served on this task force, *ex-officio*.

After several meetings with organ curator, Irv Lawless,[93] a list of recommended repairs was created that included a recommendation for the installation of an additional solo trumpet stop.

At the time this history went to press in fall 2013, the Lively-Fulcher Pipe Organ Company of Virginia had been retained to oversee the comprehensive revoicing of the instrument. Removal of pipework took place during the summer. The Walker Technical Company, which had already enhanced the organ with a few select digital stops and sounds, was engaged to add several additional voices. "Especially noteworthy will be the addition of a new Festival Trumpet," said Michael Divine, Director of Music Ministries.

---

[93] Irv Lawless was for many years responsible for the care and maintenance of the Kennedy Center organ. His parents were members of Lewinsville, and he was involved in the installation of the Lewinsville organ.

A rededication service for the organ was held September 29, 2013.

History of the Bells

Handbells at Lewinsville were made by Malmark Bellcraftsmen in Plumsteadville, Pennsylvania. The first 3-octave set was donated to Lewinsville by Nancy and Roy Mitchell in 1979 in memory of Nancy's mother, Ruth Bishop.[94] The choir's full set of equipment includes English handbells, choir chimes, padded tables, mallets, special music stands and table coverings. In all, Lewinsville owns 124 handbells (two five-octave sets) and ninety-eight choir chimes (one five-octave and one three-octave set).

A handbell choir ensemble is a group that rings recognizable music with melodies and harmony, as opposed to the mathematical permutations used in change ringing. While a smaller group uses only two octaves (twenty-five bells), the sets are often larger, ranging up to an eight-octave set (ninety-seven bells). The bells are typically arranged chromatically on foam covered tables. These tables protect the bronze surface of the bell and secure the bell in its proper place on the table. Unlike an orchestra or choir in which each musician is responsible for one line of the texture, a bell ensemble acts as one instrument, with each

---

[94] Since 1979, additional bells have been added to the original three-octave set, donated by or in honor of Waldo Bishop, Bruce Bishop, Allan Eckstein, Olive Still, Mr. and Mrs. Chester Shaw, Mr. and Mrs. Philip Maguer, Loyal and Helen Williams, Anna and James Shaw, Earl and Janet Merritt, Lynda Briscoe (Sharrett), Roy and Betty Palmer, and Lee Billups. There are inscriptions on some of the bells indicating those honored or memorialized by the gifts.

musician responsible for particular notes, sounding assigned bells whenever that note appears in the music.

The bells used in American handbell choirs are almost always English handbells. "English handbells" is a reference to a specific type of handbell, not to the country of origin. While some American handbell choirs use bells made in England, the majority perform with bells manufactured in the United States by Malmark Bellcraftsmen or by Schulmerich Carillons.

**

Appendix III

"Concerning Our New Church"[95]
November 18, 1956

Our new church at Lewinsville now stands ready to meet the growing needs of a growing community. Below are a few facts concerning our new building.

---

[95] Official program of dedication, November 18, 1956

Allen J. Dickey of Arlington served as architect and the firm of Sharpe & Hamaker Incorporated, also of Arlington, was the contractor. The building was erected on the site of the original 1846 church. Two features from the original church are incorporated in the new construction:

The old cornerstone now bears the dates 1846-1956. Sealed in a copper box in the cornerstone are: a large 1846 penny (date of the original church), $1.10 in new 1956 coins (representing our 110th year), picture of previous church cut from plate, Church History, Annual Report, list of members in 1852 (copied from old quilt), and a 1956 Yearbook.

One wall of the Fellowship Hall is wainscoted with paneling from the original church. Above the wainscoting are two sections of windows from the 1846 building, behind which are back lighted glass shelves containing relics and a written explanation of their place in the history of the church.

In size the new church is 42 by 105 feet with two full floors. Both architecture and furnishings are colonial. The bricks are a Calvert rose. Each evening the entire front of the church and steeple are illuminated by floodlights.

Only in architecture have we borrowed from the old. The Sanctuary floor is covered with cork tile, the wainscoting is white, and the walls a Sistine blue. The ceilings are covered with acoustical plaster. Antique glass is used in the rounding windows. The Chancel, which is 18 by 24 feet and covered by a cathedral red carpet, is "divided," with accommodations for 27 in the choir. The 42 by 62 foot Sanctuary has a seating capacity of 340. All of the Sanctuary and Chancel furniture is made of hard maple, and is white trimmed in walnut. Behind the Chancel is a large unfinished area which will be used for the Pastor's Study, the church secretary, and the choir rooms. Just off the vestibule a large cloakroom has been provided.

On the floor below is a Fellowship Hall, 42 by 79 feet. The Women's Association has equipped the kitchen with lovely, modern conveniences. In addition, this floor contains at the rear a boiler room and a storage room. At the front there are rest rooms and a downstairs cloakroom. There are two inside and two outside stairways. The oil furnace provides radiant heat in the downstairs floors and baseboard heat for the Sanctuary. In addition to hot water heat, the church is equipped to provide hot air heat and a rapid circulation of air. Although the actual unit has not been installed, oversized heat ducts and fans have been provided for future air conditioning.

The congregation is now ready to "Worship the Lord in the beauty of holiness."

Participants in the 1956 service of dedication:

- Rev. Franklin B. Gillespie, Pastor, 1940-1948, current Secretary, Department of Young People's Program in the Presbyterian Church USA

- Rev. James F. Lundquist, Pastor, 1948-1953, current Associate Pastor at Westminster Presbyterian Church, Alexandria, Virginia

- Rev. Ralph K. Merker, D.D., current Moderator and Stated Clerk of the Presbytery of Washington City

- Rev. Howard F. Newman, Th.D., Pastor of Lewinsville Presbyterian Church

- *Harold W. Arberg, Ed.D., Minister of Music, Lewinsville Presbyterian Church*

Appendix IV
Lewinsville Tapestry[96]

---

[96] Description on the following pages is taken from the Sesquicentennial Program, October 18-20, 1996

132 || Pilgrims and Pioneers Always

The tapestry displayed in the Narthex represents the life and heritage of Lewinsville Presbyterian Church from its founding, October 17, 1846, to the celebration of its 150th anniversary, October 18-20, 1996.

The First Church was built in 1846 and served continuously as the home of the Lewinsville congregation until 1956.
Stitcher: Carol Kaffenberger

The Singing Choirs with participants from among young children, junior and senior high school youth, and adults form an important part of the life of the church.
Stitchers: Katie Cummings and Karen Steel

The Ministry at Lewinsville encompasses Sunday morning worship services, Christian education and every facet of church life as well as outreach into the community.
Stitcher: Bettie Vodra (McElroy)

The Cemetery predates the original sanctuary and has been the final resting place for persons in the church and community for more than a century and a half.
Stitcher: Karen Steel

Appendix IV: Lewinsville Tapestry || 133

 **The Bell Choirs** have brought ringing to accompany singing in Lewinsville's music ministry and include participants ranging in age from young children to senior citizens.
Stitcher: Nancy McGuire

 **World Mission** from McLean to the greater Washington area to overseas is an important part of the ministry through PC(USA) and Lewinsville's own special forms of outreach.
Stitcher: Caroline Van Wagoner

 **The Lewinsville Retirement Residence** opened in 1980 and has been home to hundreds of senior citizens in the years since, and forms another outreach of this church to the community.
Stitcher: Anne Clare

 **The Present Church** represents a number of building efforts during the most recent forty years, including a new sanctuary, Heritage Hall, a new Narthex, St. Andrews Hall, and new offices to undertake our ministry.
Stitcher: Betty McKenna

The Lewinsville tapestry was conceived by Duane and Betty McKenna. It took nine months to create and required more than 900,000 stitches by eight workers laboring more than 5,000 hours. Tapestry was unveiled and dedicated, October 6, 1996.

**

Appendix V
Musical Productions and Cantatas

1969	April	**Let Us Follow Him** – Musical Drama
1971	June	**Sing with Joy** – Westminster Choir
1973	March	**Godspell** – Westminster Choir
1974	May/June	**Jonah** – Westminster Choir
1975	February	**Hansel and Gretel** – Intergenerational Play
	May	**Prodigal Son** – St. Francis/St. Cecilia Choirs
	May	**Tobias and the Angel** – Westminster Choir
1976	Feb/June	**Mr. Paul** – Westminster Choir
1978	May/June	**Prodigal Son** – Westminster Choir
1979	April	**Godspell** – Westminster Choir
	April/June	**Remember the Rainbow** – Westminster Choir
1980	February	**Godspell** – Westminster Choir
1981	February	**Holy Moses** – A Jazz Cantata – St., Cecilia Choir
	May	**Daniel and Friends** – Westminster Choir
1982	February	**Godspell** – Westminster Choir

	April	**Joseph and the Amazing Technicolor Dream Coat** – Westminster Choir
	May	**The Singing Bishop** (Cantata) – Cherub Choir and Rainbow Choir
	June	**Up, Up and Away** – Scotland Sabbatical Celebration
1983	February	**Captain Noah and His Floating Zoo** – Cantata – St. Cecilia Choir
	May/June	**Ruth and Naomi** – Westminster Choir
1984		**The Business Trip** – Cantata – Cherub and Genesis Choirs
1986	February/March	**A Cantata Every Sunday** – Intergenerational Cast
1988	October	**Pass the Peace** – Gary's 20th Anniversary Celebration
1989		**The Story-Tellin' Man** – Cantata – Westminster and Genesis Choirs
1991	May	**A Season to Celebrate** – Cantata – Westminster Choir
	June	**Jerome and Augustine** – Original Adult Production
1992		**A Reason to Rejoice** – Cantata – Westminster Choir
1994		**Godspell** – Westminster Choir
1995	May	**Francis: The Poor Little Man of God** – Cantata – Cherub and Genesis Choirs
1996	May	**Good Kings Come in Small Packages**
1997	June	**Rescue in the Night** – The Story of Daniel in the Lions' Den – Genesis and Cherub Choirs

Appendix V: Music Productions and Cantatas || 137

1998	February	**Bright New Wings** – Cantata – Westminster Choir
	April	**The Great Vigil of Easter**
	April	**Alleluia for the Lord, our God, the Almighty, has come into His Kingdom**
	May	**Cool in the Furnace** – Cantata – Cherub and Genesis Choirs
1999	February	**Acts** – A Choral Music Drama – Westminster Choir
	June	**The Rock Slinger and His Greatest Hit** – Cantata – Genesis and Cherub Choirs
2000	February	**Credo** – Westminster Choir
	June	**Tale of the Three Trees** – Cantata – Genesis and Cherub Choirs
2001	May	**On This Rock** – Musical Drama – Cherub and Genesis Choirs
2002	May	**Jubilee: We Are Set Free** – Cherub and Genesis Choirs
2003	February	**All God's Children** – Cherub and Genesis Choirs
2004	February	**Cool in the Furnace** – Cherub and Genesis Choirs
	June	**Gospel Mass** – Westminster and Chancel Choirs
	November	**A Reason to Rejoice** – Westminster Choir
2005	February	**Tale of the Three Trees** – Cherub and Genesis Choirs
	April	**A Festival of Doors** – Westminster and Chancel Choirs

**

Appendix VI
Return of the Original Baptismal Font[97]

The return of the original baptismal font, missing since the end of the Civil War, occurred May 12, 1996, and officially marked the opening of Lewinsville's 150th anniversary celebration.

The font was taken during the Civil War when Union troops were stationed at Lewinsville. On October 15, 1861, General Hancock of the Union forces issued an order that the church be burned if it should fall into the hands of Confederate troops. Eliza T. Wilson, who accompanied the Dunn County Pinery Rifles of the Fifth Wisconsin Regiment as a nurse, saved the baptismal font and a communion cup after she witnessed straw being spread around the church prepatory to its burning. A few months later, she returned to her home in Menominee, Wisconsin, with the font and communion cup among her belongings.

Eliza Wilson was the daughter of William Wilson, a prominent Menominee businessman and former state senator who was instrumental in organizing the Pinery Rifles. She was caught up in the intense spirit of a gathering at which her father spoke in support of the Union cause. As a result, she volunteered to accompany the military unit as a practical nurse "to share with its members the hardships of the march and to nurse them if they fell ill or were wounded."

Chaperoned by her relatives, she became a fixture of the Pinery Rifles. She was known as the Daughter of the Regiment, and according to a Dunn County Historical Association newsletter, she dressed in the

---

[97] From the Sesquicentennial Program, October 18-20, 1996 (with minor edits)

bright brown, Turkish-style uniform prescribed for nurses with the Union Army.

After the war, she became a prominent businesswoman in Menominee, and worked with a major lumber company. She was also an active feminist, playing host to Susan B. Anthony and Elizabeth Cady Stanton when they visited Menominee.

It has never been determined why she did not return the font and cup immediately after the war. The local historical society speculated that perhaps she treasured them as mementoes of her Virginia experience, or perhaps she thought the church had no interest in the items after the war. For whatever reason, she retained possession until July 31, 1895, when she presented them to the William Evans Post of the Grand Army of the Republic. From there, the font and cup passed to the Empire Pine Museum in the 1950s, a museum that chronicled the history of the Dunn County lumber industry. No one knows if the lumbermen questioned the presence of a baptismal font in their museum, or asked about its relationship to the lumber industry.

Figure 59-Rev. Gary Pinder puts the original font to use immediately upon its return, 1996 (on small table)

The Dunn County Historical Association apparently decided to return the font to Lewinsville in 1965, at the end of the centennial celebration of the Civil War, but no action was taken.

In the summer of 1977, Barbara Kriss, former member of Lewinsville, who was living in Wisconsin, learned that a bowl in a museum in Downsville, Dunn County, Wisconsin, was the long lost baptismal font of Lewinsville Presbyterian Church. She visited the museum and copied the inscription, took a picture and forwarded the information to Lewinsville. For another fifteen years, the church and the museum negotiated its return to Virginia.

Appendix VI: Return of the Original Baptismal Font || 141

And still, no action was taken.

In February 1980, church historian Frank Gapp wrote an article for *Northern Virginia Heritage*, titled, "Lewinsville's Liberated Baptismal Font." Kenneth G. Clare, a member of Lewinsville and alumnus of the University of Wisconsin, made several trips to Menominee, Wisconsin, and determined that the font and cup were still in the museum. He contacted John Russell, former president of the Dunn County Historical Association, and an effort to return the font and cup began in earnest. Rev. Pinder and elders Howard Salzman and Robert A. Alden also became involved in communications between the church and museum. As the 150th anniversary of the church approached, Bob Alden and John Russell worked out final arrangements for the font's return. Today the font is displayed in a case specifically designed for it and positioned in a place of honor outside the church office.

Return of the Original Pulpit Lamp[98]

In 1908, after Lewinsville Presbyterian Church was "electrified," the original oil-fueled pulpit lamp was retired and turned over to the family of Hunter Mack.

Hunter's parents, who first brought Hunter to Sunday School at Lewinsville in the 1890s, passed the lamp down to Hunter, and it remained with him until his death.

Hunter Mack participated in both the 100th and 125th anniversaries of the church and was on the committee that called Franklin B. Gillespie to be Lewinsville's pastor in 1940. In 1954, Hunter served as an elder-commissioner from the Washington City Presbytery to the Presbyterian U.S.A. General Assembly. An elder and

---

[98] From the Sesquicentennial Program, October 18-20, 1996 (with minor edits)

trustee of Lewinsville for many years, Hunter was Clerk of Session at the time of the centennial in 1946. He also sang in the choir and had been superintendent of the church school.

Figure 60-Hunter and Alda Mack with Sunday School children.

Hunter proudly described himself and his wife, Alda, as "young Turks who supported the concept of bringing a young, full-time minister to Lewinsville" in 1939, a discussion that caused some division within the congregation because longtime supply pastor J. Harvey Dunham had anticipated becoming Lewinsville's pastor upon his retirement from Western Presbyterian Church.

When Hunter died in 1978, Alda Mack drove to Wallingford, Pennsylvania, and presented the pulpit lamp to Rev. Gillespie, telling him that Hunter thought the lamp should go to him.

Rev. Gillespie, who presided over the 100th anniversary of the church in 1846 wrote Bob Alden, organizer and coordinator of the 150th anniversary, and offered to return the lamp to its rightful home. Gillespie had been approached by the Presbyterian Historical Society, but decided Lewinsville should have it.

With concurrence from Rev. Gary Pinder and the 150th anniversary committee, Bob Alden accepted Rev. Gillespie's offer. The handsome oil lamp was officially returned when Franklin and Marion Gillespie participated in the activities of the Sesquicentennial Weekend.

Figure 61-Gillespies in front of church, circa 1947. Children: Frank, Jr., 4 and Carolyn, 2.

Rev. Gillespie's presentation was part of the anniversary dinner program, Friday, October 19, 1996.

**

Appendix VII
Summer Mission Project – Trip History[99]
1990-2013

June 1990   Sea Island Habitat for Humanity - Johns Island, SC
Hurricane relief, including roof repair, and foundation work at a new build site as well as framing and digging a septic pump ditch.

June 1991   Sumter Habitat for Humanity - Sumter, SC
New build construction including roofing, siding and drywall.

June 1992   West Philadelphia Habitat for Humanity-Philadelphia, PA
Rehab work on city row houses, which included completely digging out a basement to re-pour the foundation concrete.

June 1993   Garrett County Habitat for Humanity - Oakland, MD
New build construction with a concentration on cement ramps for disabled and elderly homeowners.

June 1994   Pittsburgh Habitat for Humanity - Pittsburgh, PA
Demolition work on condemned city block which included removing drywall and clearing back lots. In addition, rehab work was done in another area, which included rough wiring, insulation and drywall repair.

---

[99] Source: Linda Bender, SMP Coordinator

June 1995	**Almost Heaven Habitat for Humanity - Circleville, WV** *New build construction including drywall, front and back porch construction, foundation preparation, roofing and framing.*
June 1996	**Greenville Habitat for Humanity - Greenville, SC** *New build construction including roofing, siding, drywall, landscaping and painting.*
June 1997	**Garrett County Habitat for Humanity - Oakland, MD** *New build construction including siding, drywall and framing. Also rehab work including drywall repair and painting.* **Habitat for Humanity of Greater Lynchburg - Lynchburg, VA** *New build construction including roofing, siding, drywall, landscaping and painting.*
Sept. 1997	**Habitat for Humanity of Greater Lynchburg - Lynchburg, VA** *Participated in day one of a weeklong Blitz Build which included framing and roofing of 15 houses.*
June 1998	**Garrett County Habitat for Humanity - Oakland, MD** *New build construction including siding, drywall and framing. Also rehab work including drywall repair and painting.* **Habitat for Humanity of Greater Lynchburg - Lynchburg, VA** *New build construction including roofing, siding, drywall, landscaping and painting.*

June, 1999	**Eastern Shore Virginia Habitat for Humanity – Belle Haven, VA** *New build construction including siding and drywall.* **Habitat for Humanity of Talbot County – Easton, MD** *New build construction including siding, drywall and framing. Also rehab work including drywall repair and painting.*
June 2000	**Habitat for Humanity of Greater Lynchburg – Lynchburg, VA** *Blitz Build – one house in one week, including 100% funding.*
June 2001	**Project Crossroads and Smyth County Habitat – Marion, VA** *New build construction including drywall, front and back porch construction, foundation preparation, roofing and framing.*
June 2002	**Habitat for Humanity of Greater Lynchburg – Lynchburg, VA** *New build construction including drywall, front and back porch construction, foundation preparation, roofing and framing.*
June 2003	**Garrett County Habitat for Humanity - Oakland, MD** *New build construction including foundation preparation and completion of two sheds.*
June, 2004	**East Cooper Habitat for Humanity – Isle of Palms, SC** *New build construction including framing, drywall, roofing, siding, and shed construction.*
June 2005	**Presbyterian Disaster Assistance - Fort Myers, FL** *Hurricane relief – clean-up and installing roof tarps.*

January 2006   East Cooper Habitat for Humanity – Isle of Palms, SC
** *New winter project established for college age youth and older.*** *New build construction including framing, drywall and roofing.*

June 2006   Habitat for Humanity of Washington County - Hagerstown, MD
New build construction including framing, drywall, roofing, and siding.

January 2007   Habitat for Humanity of Jacksonville - Jacksonville, FL
Interior and exterior painting.

June 2007   Homes for our Troops – Waxhaw, NC
New build construction for a local war veteran including foundation preparation and framing.

January 2008   Habitat for Humanity of Charlotte – Charlotte, NC
New build construction including framing and roofing.

June 2008   New Orleans Area Habitat for Humanity – New Orleans, LA
Hurricane relief – new build construction. Included framing one house and painting several others.

January 2009   Sea Island Habitat for Humanity - Johns Island, SC
New build construction including siding, porch work and insulation.

June 2009   Habitat for Humanity of Greater Greensboro – Greensboro, NC
Assisted homeowners with a variety of home improvement projects and also built benches, games, and bunk beds for a local YMCA camp.

Appendix VII: Summer Mission Project Trip History || 149

January 2010	**New Orleans Area Habitat for Humanity – New Orleans, LA** *Hurricane relief – new build construction.*
June 2010	**Presbyterian Disaster Assistance – Port Arthur, TX** *Hurricane relief – home improvements/repairs and painting.*
January 2011	**Darlington County Habitat for Humanity – Hartsville, SC** *New build construction (specifically framing).*
June 2011	**Darlington County Habitat for Humanity – Hartsville, SC** *New build construction – continuation of January project, including roofing and siding. Also worked with 3 other local community groups: Darlington County Humane Society, Free Medical Clinic of Darlington County, and Boys & Girls Club of Darlington County.*
January 2012	**Darlington County Habitat for Humanity – Hartsville, SC** *New build construction (specifically framing).*
Summer 2012	**Avery County Habitat for Humanity – about 45 minutes west of Boone, NC**
January 2013	**Darlington County Habitat for Humanity – Hartsville, SC**
Summer 2013	**Monmouth County, NJ** *Assisting Middletown Volunteer Corps and OceanPort Cares with Hurricane Sandy recovery*

Figure 62-New Jersey SMP 2013

Appendix VIII
Pastors, Associate Pastors, Assistant Pastors, Co-Pastors, and Stated Supplies

Name	Years of Service
Levi H. Christian, Pastor	1846-1848
F.N. Whaley (Licentiate)	1848-1852
B.F. Bittinger, Pastor	1852-1857
Charles B. McKee, Pastor	1857-1859
E.B. Smith, Pastor	1859-1861
[Visiting preachers were invited during Civil War, most notable was Rev. A.L. Taylor who served in the years of 1862 to 1865]	
Henry Snyder	1865-1866
H.P. Dechert, Stated Supply	1866-1870
David Hoge Riddle, Jr., Pastor	1871-1873
John Brown, Pastor	1873-1875
Jeremiah Odell,[100] Stated Supply	1875-1876
Samuel Murdock, Stated Supply	1876-1880
Edward H. Cumpston, Stated Supply	1880-1881
Harrison Clarke, Pastor	1881-1884
Joseph E. Nourse, Stated Supply	1885-1886
William H. Edwards, Pastor	1886-1895
French W. Fisher, Pastor	1896-1897
David W. Montgomery, Pastor	1897-1900
French W. Fisher, Pastor	1901-1903
Edward H. Bronson, Pastor	1904-1907
Nelson H. Miller, Stated Supply	1907-1912
James W. Nourse, Stated Supply	1912-1918
William R. McElroy, Pastor	1919-1923
James Harvey Dunham, Stated Supply	1923-1939
Franklin B. Gillespie, Pastor	1940-1948
James F. Lundquist, Pastor	1948-1953

---

[100] Names in bold also served Vienna Presbyterian Church

152 || Pilgrims and Pioneers Always

Howard Newman, Pastor	1954-1957
John Graham, Pastor	1957-1969
Walter H. Boyd, Assistant Pastor	1962-1965
John Graham Stevens, Assistant Pastor	1965-1968
Gary George Pinder, Associate Pastor	1968-1977
Co-Pastor	1977-1986
Pastor	1986-2005
William J. Tatum, Pastor	1971-1977
John Preston Smith III, Co-Pastor	1979-1985
S. Tad Wicker, Associate Pastor	1987-1995
*Mark L. Andrews, Parish Associate	1995-2001
Emily Berman D'Andrea, Associate Pastor	2002-present
Deborah A. McKinley, Pastor/Head of Staff	2008-present

*Dr. Andrews, although not officially "called," was a Parish Associate—pastor to all and valued colleague of Rev. Pinder. The full range of his ministry could fill a separate volume.

Figure 63-**Rev. Levi H. Christian, first pastor of Lewinsville Presbyterian Church, 1846 - 1848**

**

Appendix IX
Milestone Celebrations in the Life of Lewinsville Presbyterian Church

1946 – 100th anniversary
   Pastors participating:
      Rev. Franklin B. Gillespie (1940-1948)
      [Rev. Edward H. Bronson (1904-1907), although not in attendance, was acknowledged as the only former pastor alive at the time of the anniversary.][101]

1986 – 140th anniversary
   Pastors participating:
      Rev. Franklin B. Gillespie (1940-1948)
      Rev. John Graham (1957-1969)
      Rev. Gary G. Pinder (1968-2005)
      Rev. William J. Tatum (1971-1977)
      Rev. John P. Smith III (1979-1985)

Figure 64-(Left to Right: Pastors Gillespie, Tatum, Pinder, Graham, Smith; at table is first DCE Yvonne Greatwood, 1986

---

[101] Ibid., *A Brief History*, p. 15

1990 – 144th Anniversary
    Pastors participating:
        Rev. John Graham (1957-1969)
        Rev. Gary G. Pinder (1968 - 2005)
        Rev. S. Tad Wicker, Associate Pastor (1987 - 1995)

1996 – 150th Anniversary
    Pastors participating:
        Rev. Teri Thomas, General Presbyter, National Capital Presbytery, preaching
        Rev. Gary G. Pinder (1968-2005)
        Rev. Franklin B. Gillespie (1940-1948), read Old Testament Lesson and presented the original pulpit lamp to the congregation. The lamp came to his possession through the family of Hunter Mack where it had been kept safe for 100 years.
        Rev. James Lundquist (1948-1953), led the congregation in Prayers of the People

        **

Appendix X
Clerks of Session 1922 – 2013

W.D. Weller	1922-1927
Ulysses E. Blair	1927-1930
J. Hunter Mack	1930-1950
Raymond S. Hall	1950
J. Hunter Mack	1951-1953
Raymond S. Hall	1953-1954
Frank W. Schattschneider	1954-1960
Wilfred Dean, Jr.	1960-1963
William G. McIlhiney	1963-1967
Thomas R. Estes	1967-1968
Darrell Burnett	1968-1970
Robert A. Alden	1970-1971
R.F. Watson	1971
Page L. Ingraham	1971-1974
Delmar H. Evans	1974-1975
Roy S. Mitchell	1975-1976
Robert W. Gaugler	1976 (mil. trsfr)
W. Dean, Jr.	1976-1977
William L. Siple	1977-1978
Patricia A. Robertson	1978-1979
Nancy B. Mitchell	1979-1980
Lindsey B. Herd, Jr.	1980-1981
Betty A. Marshall	1981-1982
Ruth Thomas	May 1, 1981 – April 30, 1984
Jane Arnold	May 1, 1984 – April 30, 1987
Bettie Vodra (McElroy)	May 1, 1987 – April 30, 1990
Barbara Gibby	May 1, 1990 – April 30, 1993
Stephany Crosby	May 1, 1993 – April 30, 1996

156 || Pilgrims and Pioneers Always

Carol Kaffenberger   May 1, 1996 – April 30, 1999
William Ledman   May 1, 1999 – April 30, 2002
Harriet Hopkins   May 1, 2002 – April 30, 2005
Mary Ann Ledman   May 1, 2005 – April 30, 2009
Betty Douglass   May 1, 2009 – April 30, 2012
Mary Ann Philipp   May 1, 2012 – present   -

Figure 65-Former Clerks (left to right back row): Ruth Thomas, Bettie Vodra (McElroy), Stephany Crosby, Barbara Pinder (honorary clerk), Carol Kaffenberger. (Left to right front row): Barbara Gibby, Jane Arnold

Appendix XI
1852 Friendship Quilt

The 1852 Friendship Quilt was presented to Rev. B. F. Bittinger, May 30, 1852, just six years after the founding of Lewinsville Presbyterian Church. The members and their families are recorded on the quilt in indelible ink. On the bottom of the quilt is an inscription of dedication. In some instances, the name of the farm or estate where the member resided is included.

Figure 66-1852 Friendship Quilt

Figure 67-Inscription of the 1852 Friendship Quilt: "Reverend Bittinger, Installed Pastor of the Lewinsville Presbyterian Church, May 30, 1852"

Figure 68-"Mrs. Martha C. Ball, Woodbury"

Appendix XI: 1852 Friendship Quilt || 159

On the edge of the quilt is written:
*And they that are wise shall shine as the brightness of the firmament;
And they that turn many to righteousness as the stars for ever and ever.
Daniel 12:3*

Figure 69- "Mr. G.B. Phillips, Linvale"

Contributions in support of the printing of this publication were made:

To honor the ministry of
The Reverend Dr. Mark L. Andrews
Parish Associate, 1995 to 2001
by
Robert and Joyce Johnson

To honor the 37-year ministry of
The Reverend Gary G. Pinder,
Pastor, 1968 to 2005
and now, Pastor Emeritus
by
Roland and Bettie McElroy

To honor the Music Ministry of
J. Franklin Clark, 1967 to 2004
and
Dr. Edward Alan Moore, 2005 to 2010
by
Roy and Nancy Mitchell

To honor the ministry and service
of all the "saints," past, present and future,
to Lewinsville Presbyterian Church
by
Paul and Rosalind Phillips